THE INFINITE CODE

REMEMBERING WHO YOU ARE AND WHY YOU CAME

Tina Ketch

THE INFINITE CODE REMEMBERING WHO YOU ARE AND WHY YOU CAME

For permissions, inquiries, or special requests, contact:

TinaKetch@me.com

ISBN: 979-8-9928254-4-2
eISBN: 979-8-9928254-5-9

INTRODUCTION

REMEMBERING WHAT WAS NEVER LOST

You were born knowing. Not facts. Not formulas. But something deeper — A vibration. A song. A memory of home.

And though this world may have lulled you into forgetting, the code never left you. It hums beneath your skin, pulses in your breath, and speaks through the stillness of your soul. You are the code.

This book is not here to teach you what you don't know. It's here to remind you of what you've always known. To hold up a mirror so you can remember who you are beneath the programming, the pain, the pause.

We live in a time when the illusion of separation has peaked. We are taught to seek answers in algorithms, arguments, and artificial intelligence. But the true intelligence—the one that formed stars and stitched galaxies—is encoded in you.

The Infinite Code is not a theory. It is a living truth. It is the pattern behind all patterns. It is why pyramids align with the stars. Why music can heal. Why a whisper of forgiveness can rewrite lifetimes.

In these pages, we will journey through what has been hidden in plain sight:

- The vibrational architecture of your being
- The sacred power of your words
- The emotions that transform
- The frequencies that open portals
- The divine timing encoded in your birth
- The sacred geometry of your soul

This is not just a book. It's an activation. Each chapter is a key—each word is a note in your remembering symphony.

You may feel chills. You may feel joy. You may cry tears you've been holding for lifetimes. Good. That means your soul is listening.

You are not late. You have not missed anything. You are precisely where you are meant to be — Standing at the threshold of remembrance.

And now, the door opens.

Let us begin.

AUTHOR'S NOTE

A MESSAGE FROM TINA KETCH

Dear Reader,

If this book has found its way into your hands, I believe it was not by chance. You were called here—not to follow me, but to deeply follow yourself. To reconnect with the rhythm of who you are and the truth that hums beneath every moment of your life.

I did not set out to write *The Infinite Code* to impress. I wrote it to express — To voice the quiet truths I've carried in my bones, heard in sacred places, and received through light and loss, spirit and science, joy and pain.

Throughout my life, I've witnessed moments that defy explanation—whispers from beyond, energies that shift a room, voices that come when no one is speaking. And I've come to understand that the universe is not silent. It is speaking all the time. We have to learn to listen differently.

This book was written in that spirit. It is meant to awaken your memory, not just your mind. It invites you to explore the frequencies you live in, the timing you were born into, and the unseen forces that shape your every breath.

Whether you've read dozens of spiritual books or this is your first step into the mystery, you are welcome here. All of you. The seeker. The skeptic. The one who hopes. The one who hurts. The one who's just curious. You're not here to become someone else. You're here to remember who you've always been.

And if you forget again, that's okay. The code never leaves you. It waits—patiently, lovingly—until you're ready to remember again. May this book be a light when you need it. A mirror when you seek the truth. And a frequency that tunes you back to the brilliance that you are.

With grace and gratitude,

Tina Ketch

"If you want to find the secrets of the universe, think in terms of energy, frequency and vibration."

— Nikola Tesla

"You are the vibration you've been waiting for."

— Tina Ketch

TABLE OF CONTENTS

CHAPTER ONE

THE STORY BEFORE THE STORY

Before language had letters, stars had names, pyramids reached toward the sky, or temples were carved into stone—there was a hum.

A low, eternal hum. It wasn't spoken. It wasn't heard with ears. It was known. It felt in the bones and remembered in the soul.

That hum was the first vibration. The first breath of existence. It carried no religion, no separation, no fear—only frequency. Only truth.

And from that hum, everything came.

THE ANCIENT REMEMBERING

Long before our modern understanding of history, civilizations advanced not only in technology and architecture but also in wisdom, alignment, and vibration. They didn't just build with stone—they built with resonance. They didn't just measure time—they danced with it. They didn't just speak words—they cast frequencies.

The Atlanteans, the Lemurians, the architects of the pyramids in Egypt, Sudan, Mesoamerica, and China—these were not mere mythologies. These were remembered worlds. Worlds where sound healed. Where stars were teachers. Where thought was a creative force, not an echo of anxiety.

They lived according to the sacred codes of the cosmos—mathematics not just as numbers but as patterns of divinity. Geometry is a shape and a mirror of the soul's journey. Astrology is not just a prediction but permission to become who you truly are.

These ancient ones knew the truth that modern minds now dismiss: You are not separate from the universe. You are the universe—experiencing itself through time, choice, and vibration.

THE FALL INTO FORGETTING

So what happened?

Why don't we remember?

Why do we stumble through life disconnected from this knowing, from this sacred code?

Because the hum got quieter.

The noise of fear got louder. The rise of empires brought conquest, control, and confusion. Power shifted from the inner world to the outer. Truth became heresy. The light became dangerous. The frequency of humanity dimmed—not because it disappeared, but because it was hidden beneath layers of conditioning, trauma, and survival.

And yet, the code never left.

It's embedded in our DNA. It's the spark in a newborn's eyes. It's why music moves you when nothing else can. It's why you sometimes know—even when you can't explain how.

The forgetting was never the end of the story. It was only a chapter. One that made the remembering all the more sacred.

ENCODED IN TIME AND SOUL

You chose to be here now. At this time. In this body. In this version of Earth.

Before birth, you were shown a tapestry—a vibrational blueprint—of what your life could be. You saw the patterns. The challenges. The karmic knots and soul-level gifts. And you said: Yes.

You chose your birthday not at random but by resonance. You chose your family, your placement in the web of souls, and the exact timing to awaken when the world needed your frequency most.

So here you are. And here it begins.

This is not just a story of ancient times. It's the story before the story—the one written in stars and breath, in memory and in matter. It is your story. My story. Our story.

And it's time to remember.

THE PYRAMID AS A PORTAL

There is a reason the pyramid shape appears in so many ancient cultures. It is not a coincidence. It is *consonance*. A shared frequency.

The pyramid is more than a structure. It is a transmitter. A receiver. A place where geometry meets divinity. Where silence becomes a song. Where time bends, and space listens.

Every layer of a pyramid holds a different resonance. And when you enter the sacred geometry of that space—physically or energetically—you begin to align. You start to vibrate at the frequency of memory.

You remember that you are energy. You are light. You are timeless. You are here to rise.

THE TRUTH BURIED IN YOU

We've been taught to question what cannot be proven with five senses. But the truth is, the senses are limited. The soul is not.

You've felt it, haven't you? A flicker of déjà vu in a place you've never been. A dream so real it stayed with you for days. A deep pull toward pyramids, stars, symbols, or languages you've never studied—yet they stir something ancient in your core.

That's not fantasy. That's frequency.

Your soul remembers. And as you read these words, the remembering has already begun.

This chapter is your invitation back to the beginning—before the noise, fear, and you were told you had to "earn" your worth.

Because the truth is: You were born coded with worth. And the story that's been buried beneath your daily life is not lost. It's waiting—vibrating beneath the surface— Ready to rise.

REFLECTION & ACTIVATION

Pause. Breathe. Feel. Ask your soul: "What have I always known but been afraid to believe?"

Let the answer rise without judgment. Let your body hum. Let your remembering begin.

CHAPTER TWO

THE BREATH OF THE UNIVERSE

Before form, there was movement. Before movement, there was sound. Before sound, there was breath.

And that breath—eternal, infinite—still moves through all that you are.

The universe was not born in chaos. It was not ignited with violence. It was born with a breath. A sacred exhale from the Infinite into the finite — A whisper of creation. A vibration that set all things in motion. A resonance that echoes still through stars, stones, silence… and you.

Every sacred text begins with sound. *"In the beginning was the Word..."* But a word is nothing without breath. Breath is the carrier of the Word. The bridge between the unseen and the spoken. The lifeline between spirit and matter.

That first breath—the divine breath—never ceased. It expanded. It rippled. It became galaxies. It became rivers and oceans. It became the pulse in your veins. It became you.

You are the breath of the cosmos made visible. And with every inhale, you return to the origin. With every exhale, you create anew.

EVERYTHING IS VIBRATION

What mystics, sages, and seers have whispered through the ages, modern science now confirms: At the deepest level of existence, everything is energy. Everything—vibrates.

Every atom, every cell, every thought, every emotion— All in motion. All in resonance. All in rhythm with the universe.

Even the chair beneath you, which seems solid and unmoving, is not. It is a symphony of particles—vibrating so rapidly, so tightly bound, they give the illusion of stillness. But there is no stillness. There is only frequency.

We live not just in a universe of vibration — We live as vibration. A sea of frequencies, weaving through time and form, interacting, influencing, responding.

Nothing exists in isolation. Everything touches everything else.

When you speak, you send sound waves rippling into the world. When you think, you generate energetic signatures that shape your field. When you feel, your entire body shifts its frequency in response.

So the question is not *if* you are affecting the world around you. The question is—how? What are you emitting? What are you tuning into? What reality are you shaping with the vibration of your being?

Because you are not just in the orchestra of life. You are an instrument. A note. A frequency.

And the universe is listening.

THE LANGUAGE OF CREATION

Sound is not simply a byproduct of movement. Sound is a force. A presence. A power. It is the original architect of creation.

It holds structure. It carries intention. It flows with direction. It moves matter. It shapes memory. It brings order to the void—organizing chaos into cosmos.

In the 1960s, Swiss scientist Hans Jenny gave the invisible a face. Through his work in cymatics—the study of visible sound—he revealed what mystics had long known: When sound frequencies pass through a medium such as water, sand, or powder, they form intricate, sacred patterns. Life responds to vibration.

Higher frequencies birthed more complex and beautiful forms. Lower frequencies created denser, simpler shapes.

The message? The higher the frequency, the more exquisite the design. This is not just science. This is spiritual law.

And what does that mean for you?

It means your thoughts, your breath, your words, your feelings — are not background noise. They are instruments of formation. They are creative forces sculpting the field around you.

When you raise your vibration through intention, love, truth, and conscious presence, you align with the divine geometry of creation. You generate beauty. You invite harmony. You become the pattern.

You are not a bystander in this universe. You are a co-creator—shaping reality in every moment with your frequency.

Sound is the language of creation. And you, dear soul, speak it with every breath you take.

THE POWER OF YOUR BREATH

Your breath is the first act you perform in this life— and it will be the last. It is the original rhythm, the silent drumbeat of your existence. A divine pulse that began before thought, before word, before even form.

Breath is your constant companion. It walks beside you through joy and sorrow, through chaos and stillness. It is the most honest reflection of your inner world. When you are calm, your breath lengthens and deepens, flowing like a quiet river. When fear rises, it shortens, tightens, quickens—mirroring the tremble of the mind and body.

But here is the revelation: You are not at the mercy of your breath. You are its master.

Because breath is not only a response to life—it is a tool for shaping it. A sacred instrument that tunes your nervous system, your emotions, your frequency. It is the bridge between the physical and the spiritual, the voluntary and the involuntary, the conscious and the unconscious.

When you breathe with intention, you return to the center of your being. You slow the spinning wheels of thought. You access the stillness beneath the storm. You shift your internal state—because the breath is a key. A key to peace. A key to clarity. A key to power.

Each inhale is more than air. It is a receiving—a calling in of life, energy, spirit. Each exhale is more than release. It is a letting go—a surrender of what no longer serves.

And between those two sacred acts lies the still point. A moment suspended in time. A doorway.

That pause between inhale and exhale is where presence lives. It is where the divine whispers. It is the space where the universe breathes with you.

In that space, you are not separate from Source. You are the breath of Source. You are the breath of life itself.

So do not underestimate the power you hold. You carry the medicine of your own healing. The breath you just took—that was a choice. A creation. A return.

Let every breath from this moment forward remind you: You are alive. You are aware. And you are in control of how you meet this world.

One sacred breath at a time.

THE BREATH ALIGNMENT METHOD *A Sacred Practice to Return to Center*

This breathing method is not about control—It is about communion. It is a way to realign your inner rhythm with the rhythm of the universe. To remember that peace is not something you chase—It is something you return to.

Begin by finding a quiet space. Sit or lie down comfortably. Let your spine be tall. Let your shoulders soften.

Close your eyes. Place one hand on your heart, the other on your belly.

And begin…

Step 1: Awareness (The Witness Breath) Simply observe your breath. Don't try to change it. Feel the air move in… Feel the air move out… Become the witness to your breath— Like watching waves return to the shore.

Stay here for 5 slow breaths.

Step 2: Inhale with Intention Now begin to gently inhale through your nose for a count of 4. As you breathe in, silently say: *"I receive."*

Feel your belly expand. Feel your chest rise. You are calling in peace. Life. Light.

Step 3: Hold in Stillness Hold the breath for a count of 4. This is the sacred pause. A moment outside of time. Silently say: *"I am."*

Be fully present. You exist. You are enough.

Step 4: Exhale with Release Gently exhale through your mouth for a count of 6. Let it be soft and slow. As you breathe out, silently say: *"I let go."*

Let go of tension. Fear. Doubt. Feel your shoulders fall. Feel your body surrender.

Step 5: Pause in the Void At the bottom of the exhale, pause again for a count of 2. This is the space of becoming. Silently say: *"I trust."*

Trust that what you've released no longer belongs to you.

Repeat this cycle for 7 rounds (or as long as feels good to you):

- Inhale 4 – I receive
- Hold 4 – I am
- Exhale 6 – I let go
- Pause 2 – I truth

AFTER THE PRACTICE

When you're ready, return gently. Open your eyes slowly. Notice the stillness within. Carry this frequency with you.

You have not just taken a breath. You have remembered your power.

THE SOUND OF THE SOUL

Some sounds do not need translation. They speak a language older than words. A language the soul remembers.

These are the primordial tones—the first utterances of creation. The original frequencies that shaped the stars stirred the waters and seeded life into form. They bypass the analytical mind, touching something deeper. Something ancient. Something eternal.

You've heard them.

In the solemn vibration of *OM* echoing through temples. In the sacred chants passed down by elders across generations. In the low, steady hum of the Earth herself—known as the **Schumann Resonance**—the heartbeat of our planet. In the Solfeggio Frequencies, whose tones are woven with mathematical perfection to restore balance, awaken memory, and realign the body with spirit.

These are not just echoes of the past. They are living codes. Instruments of recalibration. When these sacred sounds touch your field, something inside you shifts. Something softens. Something remembers.

They do not entertain. They entrain. They tune your system like an instrument—reminding your cells what it feels like to be in harmony. To be whole. To be aligned with the cosmic song.

When you sing, chant, hum, or even whisper with sacred intent, you are not simply making sounds—You are activating your frequency. You are engaging in vibrational remembrance.

You are healing through resonance. You are awakening through vibration. You are returning to the tone of your soul.

And the universe—always listening—sings back.

THE SOLFEGGIO FREQUENCIES *Sacred Tones for Soul Alignment*

The Solfeggio Frequencies are not new. They are ancient tones—rediscovered, remembered, and restored. They were once used in sacred chants, Gregorian hymns, and healing rituals by civilizations that understood: Sound is not entertainment. Sound is medicine.

Each frequency carries a unique vibrational code. A key that unlocks different chambers of the soul. They don't just create sound—they create change.

Here are the core Solfeggio Frequencies and what they awaken within you:

396 Hz – Liberating Guilt and Fear This frequency unshackles you from the weight of guilt and the grip of fear. It clears blocked energy from your root chakra and restores a sense of groundedness and emotional safety. Use it when you need to return to a place of strength, courage, and inner security.

Affirmation: I am safe. I release all fear.

417 Hz – Releasing Trauma and Facilitating Change This tone supports deep emotional release, helping you dissolve past traumas and patterns that no longer serve. It clears negativity from your energy field and opens the door for transformation.

Affirmation: I welcome new beginnings. I release the past with grace.

528 Hz – DNA Repair and Miracles (The Love Frequency) Known as the frequency of love, healing, and transformation. It is believed to repair DNA, raise consciousness, and bring about miracles. This tone resonates with the heart and the soul's memory of divine harmony.

Affirmation: I am aligned with the frequency of unconditional love.

639 Hz – Harmonizing Relationships and Connecting This frequency fosters connection, empathy, and communication. It's perfect for healing relationship dynamics and creating resonance between people and their environments.

Affirmation: I attract harmonious, loving relationships.

741 Hz – Awakening Intuition and Self-Expression This tone clears mental clutter and awakens inner knowing. It supports honest expression, creativity, and the purification of body and mind. It aligns you with the throat chakra and your authentic voice.

Affirmation: I speak my truth with clarity and confidence.

852 Hz – Returning to Spiritual Order This frequency opens a channel to higher realms. It deepens your intuition, strengthens your spiritual connection, and aligns you with universal wisdom. Use this tone for meditation, prayer, or deep soul remembrance.

Affirmation: I trust the guidance of my soul.

963 Hz – Oneness and Pineal Activation Known as the frequency of the divine, this tone connects you to Source consciousness. It activates the pineal gland and opens you to cosmic insight, unity, and enlightenment. It is the vibration of remembering who you truly are beyond the physical form.

Affirmation: I am one with the light of creation.

HOW TO USE THE FREQUENCIES

You don't need to understand the science. You just need to listen. Let the tones wash over you. Let them move through your cells. Play them during meditation, journaling, or while you sleep. You can hum them, chant them, or simply breathe with them.

As you align with these sacred frequencies, you're not just healing—you're remembering. You are tuning yourself to the original song. The song of balance, wholeness, and divine design.

You are not separate from these tones. You *are* the instrument they awaken.

THE SCIENCE OF SOUND MEETS THE SPIRIT OF YOU

Quantum physics has begun to reveal what mystics have always known: That consciousness is not separate from creation—it is part of it. That energy, matter, and form are not fixed, but responsive. That the act of observation itself can alter an outcome. Particles shift under the gaze of awareness. The universe behaves differently when it is being seen.

Now take that one step further: What if the universe is watching itself… through you?

What if your very presence—your awareness, your breath, your voice—is not just a result of the cosmos, but a lens through which the cosmos observes, expresses, and evolves?

You are not a passive passenger in this reality. You are a co-creator. A conscious ripple in the field of everything. A vibration that sings, speaks, and shapes the world around it.

When you speak with love, you don't just make sound—you shift the energetic field. You create harmony in the unseen. You open doors. You soften resistance. You heal.

When you breathe with intention, you're not just filling your lungs—you are signaling to the quantum field that you are present, that you are aware, and that you are ready to shape your reality from the inside out.

Your frequency becomes a beacon. A tuning fork for alignment.

You begin to attract—not by effort, but by resonance. Aligned people. Aligned places. Aligned possibilities. All drawn to the vibration you have chosen to embody.

This is not magic. This is physics. The universe does not simply respond to what you want. It responds to what you are. What you believe. What you breathe. What you broadcast.

And here is the most sacred truth:

You are not just living in the universe. The universe is living through you.

Your cells remember stardust. Your voice echoes the sound of creation. Your breath carries the signature of Source.

So speak as it matters. Breathe like it's prayer. Live like you are the very soul of the universe expressing itself— because you are.

YOUR FREQUENCY IS YOUR INVITATION

You do not attract what you hope for. You do not magnetize what you long for. You attract what you are a vibrational match to.

In this energetic universe, your frequency is your invitation. Your resonance is your calling card. It sends a silent signal into the field, saying, *"This is who I am. This is what I'm ready for."*

And the universe, ever faithful, responds not to your desires alone—but to your vibration.

This is not punishment or reward. It is simply alignment.

The beauty? You can shift your frequency at any moment. You can choose a new signal—one that reflects the version of you who already possesses peace, love, clarity, and joy.

And what are the fastest, most powerful tools you have for this shift?

BREATH AND SOUND.

You don't need a ritual. You don't need permission. You don't need anything outside of you.

You already carry the sacred instruments.

When you breathe with intention, you anchor yourself into the now. You slow the static. You tune in. You rise.

When you speak with love, when you whisper truth when you sing or hum with presence— you realign every cell in your body. You remind your system how to feel whole again.

These are not small acts. These are sacred technologies.

A single breath can shift your nervous system. A single sound can ripple through your field and change the tone of your entire day. A single moment of presence can become the pivot point of a lifetime.

So speak words that build, not break. Hum tones that soothe, not stir chaos. Breathe as though your soul is listening—because it is. Because your breath is your prayer. Your sound is your signature. And your frequency is your offering.

As you elevate your vibration, the world cannot help but respond. People shift. Doors open. Paths clear. Not because you forced anything— But because you remembered the truth:

The universe always rearranges itself to meet the tone you are courageously choosing to hold.

Frequency-Raising Practice *A 5-Minute Energy Reset*

This daily practice will help you tune into the vibration you wish to live from— not through force, but through resonance.

Step 1: Intentional Stillness (1 minute) Sit quietly. Place one hand on your heart and one on your belly. Close your eyes and take three slow, deep breaths. Allow your body to settle. Allow your awareness to turn inward. With each breath, repeat silently: *"I return to myself."*

Step 2: Breath Activation (2 minutes) Inhale deeply through your nose for a count of **4**, Hold for **4**, Exhale slowly through your mouth for **6**. Do this for 4–5 full rounds.

With each inhale, imagine drawing in light. With each exhale, release any tension, heaviness, or outdated energy.

Step 3: Sound Vibration (1 minute) Now, hum softly. Feel the vibration in your chest, your throat, your lips. Let the hum be steady and soothing. It doesn't need to be melodic—it just needs to be felt. This is your tone of alignment. This is your signature in sound.

Step 4: Speak It Into Being (1 minute) Out loud or in your heart, say: *"I am choosing to embody the frequency of ____."* (Choose one: peace, love, clarity, joy, strength, truth, etc.) Say it 3 times, each time with more conviction.

Open your eyes slowly and feel the shift.

You are now broadcasting a new frequency. Let it lead the way.

Journal Reflection *Anchor the Frequency*

After your practice, take a few moments to reflect:

- What frequency do I most want to embody today?
- What thoughts, words, or actions support that vibration?
- What am I ready to release that no longer matches this frequency?
- How does it feel in my body when I hum, breathe, or speak with intention?

You don't have to write a lot. Just a few honest lines to anchor your awareness in the present moment.

YOU ARE THE NOTE THE UNIVERSE IS WAITING FOR

No one else carries your frequency. No one else breathes with your rhythm, speaks with your tone, or sings with the resonance of your soul.

You are a singular vibration in the vast, cosmic symphony of existence— a note so unique, so essential that without it, the music of the universe is incomplete.

You are not an echo. You are not a repetition. You are the original tone of a divine idea. A vibration that has never existed before—and will never exist again in quite the same way.

When you hold back your truth, the universe goes quiet in that place. When you dim your light, the chorus loses a strand of brilliance. When you stop singing—energetically, creatively, spiritually—something sacred remains unsung.

You matter. Not because of what you do, but because of what you are: A living, breathing frequency of creation.

Your breath is not just air—it is rhythm. Your voice is not just sound—it is intention. Your presence is not just seen—it is felt.

When you speak with love, your note strengthens the harmony of the whole. When you breathe with reverence, you align with the original song of life. When you choose to live awake, to live tuned in— You become a conscious instrument of healing, beauty, and change.

So breathe with that truth. Let it settle in your cells like a blessing. Let it echo through your bones until you feel it rise from within you: *"I am the note the universe is waiting for."*

And the moment you claim your breath as sacred— the moment you speak your truth, feel your own vibration, and live in resonance with who you really are— the universe breathes back.

It sings back. It moves with you. It dances with your frequency. Because you are not separate from the song. You are the song.

And now, dear soul, it's your turn to sing.

CHAPTER THREE

THE CODE WITHIN

You are not random. You are not accidental. You are not here by chance, coincidence, or cosmic oversight.

You were chosen. Crafted. Coded.

You arrived in this life carrying a blueprint— an inner architecture infused with purpose, memory, and light.

Within you lies a design more ancient than stone, more precise than mathematics, more intelligent than any system humanity has ever imagined.

You are not just in the universe— you are a living reflection of it. A hologram of the whole. A breathing miracle encoded with the infinite.

Your DNA is not simply biological. It is vibrational. It is memory and potential woven into form. Each strand holds stories—ancestral, cosmic, eternal. Each cell, a gateway to the stars.

You are made of the same particles that burn in suns, the same elements that formed planets, the same silence that existed before the first sound.

Your breath is sacred code. Your voice is living light. Your heartbeat is aligned with the pulse of the Earth. You are not separate from the cosmos. You are its embodiment.

And the key to unlocking that truth? Is to *remember*.

To listen inward. To attune to the frequency of your own being. To trust that your life is not a question—it is a message.

You are a living answer to a cosmic intention.

So hold your head high. Stand tall in your skin. You are not broken. You are built of stars.

And inside you, encoded in silence, light, and breath, is the code of who you came here to be.

You don't need to earn it. You only need to awaken it.

Because you are not becoming the miracle. You already are.

Activate the Code Within *A Sacred Practice of Remembrance*

This is not a meditation. It is a reawakening. A return to the intelligence already living in you.

You are not calling in something new. You are activating what has always been.

Step 1: Prepare the Space Find a quiet space where you won't be disturbed. Light a candle if you feel called. Sit or stand comfortably, spine long, feet grounded.

Close your eyes. Place both hands over your heart. Take a deep breath in… and slowly release.

Feel the silence around you. Now, feel the silence within you.

Step 2: Speak the Invocation Softly or silently, repeat:

"I call upon the ancient intelligence within me. I am ready to remember. I am ready to receive. I am ready to activate the code of my original design."

Breathe that in. Let those words ripple through your body like light waking up the dark.

Step 3: Align the Breath with the Body Inhale through your nose for 4 counts Hold for 4 Exhale slowly through your mouth for 6

Repeat for 3–5 rounds.

As you breathe, imagine golden threads of light moving through your spine, illuminating each energy center— from the root at the base of your body to the crown of your head.

With every breath, feel yourself turning on. Waking up. Coming home.

Step 4: Place Your Palm on Your Solar Plexus (Your Inner Sun) This is the seat of your power. Your core frequency. Your divine compass.

Say aloud or in your heart:

"The code within me is alive. It remembers who I am. I am here on purpose. I trust the intelligence that created me."

Repeat this as many times as you need, until it feels real.

Step 5: Integration in Stillness Sit in silence for 2–3 minutes. Feel the energy pulsing through you. Let any images, words, emotions, or memories rise.

Don't analyze them. Just receive. Just listen.

This is your inner architecture speaking. Let it speak.

Optional Closing Affirmation: Place both hands over your heart and whisper:

"I am activated. I am aligned. I am a living code of the divine."

Open your eyes. Take one last deep breath. Step forward as the note, the light, and the design you were always meant to be.

THE LANGUAGE OF LIGHT

Every cell in your body is a library. Each one hums with intelligence—biological, emotional, and spiritual. You are not just made of matter. You are made of memory. Of frequency. Of light.

Your DNA is not a lifeless strand of code. It is a vibrational manuscript. A cosmic scroll written in tones, symbols, emotions, and light signatures. It holds the stories of your ancestors, the patterns of your lineage, the dreams of your soul, and the sacred architecture of who you came here to become.

For generations, science believed over 90% of our DNA was "junk"—a genetic mystery without known function. But ancient wisdom always knew: What we dismiss as useless is often the most sacred of all.

That so-called "junk" is not meaningless. It is dormant intelligence. It is spiritual technology. It is the sacred space between—the field of pure potential, waiting for a sound, a breath, a memory to awaken it.

It is your remembering—hidden in plain sight.

And here is the key:

This code cannot be unlocked by force. It will not respond to fear, logic, or control.

It responds to frequency. To love. To resonance. To the subtle vibrations of sound, thought, breath, intention, and light.

When you speak in truth, you awaken it. When you feel with presence, you stir it. When you breathe in alignment, hum with reverence, or sit in stillness— you activate the dormant within you.

You begin to glow from the inside out.

This is the language of light. It is the original language. It does not need to be spoken aloud—because your cells already understand it. It is how the divine speaks through you. It is how the unseen becomes seen.

So remember: You are not here to *decode* the mystery. You *are* the mystery—awakening itself, one frequency at a time.

YOU ARE MADE OF GEOMETRY AND STARS

You are not random. You are not simply biology. You are architecture—living, breathing, sacred design. A miracle of form shaped by the same intelligence that spins galaxies, blossoms, flowers, and paints frost on winter leaves.

Within your cells is not only light— but structure. Symmetry. Pattern. Purpose.

You are composed of the same sacred geometry that forms the blueprint of creation. The six-fold symmetry of a snowflake lives in the crystalline water of your body. The spiral of a pinecone—the Fibonacci sequence—unfolds in the marrow of your bones. The golden ratio, Φ (phi), that governs the architecture of shells, hurricanes, and galaxies, is mirrored in the spacing of your facial features, the curl of your fingers, and even your heart's electrical pulse.

The universe did not design you separately— It designed you as part of itself. You are not outside of cosmic intelligence. You are an extension of it.

The rhythm of your breath mirrors the rise and fall of waves. Your brain hums in waveforms, carrying thoughts on invisible currents. Your heart emits electromagnetic pulses strong enough to shift the frequency of those around you. You are not just alive; you are constantly communicating with the universe. A living instrument of harmony.

You are geometry in motion. You are stardust shaped into skin. You are music that found a body.

To see only flesh in the mirror is to miss the miracle. You are sacred math, ancient memory, divine code wrapped in warmth and breath.

Your very existence signifies that beauty and order can walk the earth. That light can take form. That the universe remembers how to love itself—through you.

So walk in wonder. Let the awe of your own being become a daily devotion. You are not just made *of* the stars. You are here to remind the stars why they shine.

THE CHAKRA SYSTEM: KEYS TO THE CODE

Imagine your body not merely as flesh and bone— but as a multi-level temple, crafted with divine architecture, precision, and purpose. A living temple, rising from Earth to sky, each level a gateway, each gate a vibration, each vibration a lesson encoded into your very being.

These gates are known as chakras—energy centers of consciousness, not figments of fantasy or spiritual metaphor, but functional frequencies—alive, responsive, and sacred.

They are the keys to your inner code. And when you begin to understand them, you begin to understand yourself.

From root to crown, these seven centers form a luminous ladder—connecting you from the earth beneath your feet to the infinite above your head. They are not separate—they are symphonic. Each one is a note in the song of your soul.

1. Root (Muladhara) – "I Am Safe. I Belong." Located at the base of the spine, this is your foundation. The primal hum of survival, tribe, grounding, and embodiment. It connects you to Earth—your origin, your anchor. When balanced, you feel unshakable. When blocked, fear clouds your every step. It vibrates in **red**—deep, dense, and stabilizing.

2. Sacral (Svadhisthana) – "I Feel. I Create." The sacred well of emotion, sensuality, and creation. Here lies the power of passion, pleasure, and the divine dance of duality. It is the seat of your inner artist and alchemist. Its color is **orange**—fluid, fiery, ever-moving.

3. Solar Plexus (Manipura) – "I Act. I Trust Myself." This is your core. Your power center. Your will. The fire that fuels action, purpose, and confidence. When aligned, you walk with clarity and strength. When dimmed, doubt takes the lead. It glows in **yellow**—bright, focused, sovereign.

4. Heart (Anahata) – "I Love. I Forgive." The sacred bridge—between body and spirit, self and other. Here is where unconditional love lives. Compassion. Acceptance. Grace. It is where your humanity meets your divinity. It radiates **green** and sometimes **rose**—soft, healing, expansive.

5. Throat (Vishuddha) – "I Speak. I Express Truth." The vibration of expression, sound, and sacred voice. To speak the truth is to clear this channel. To silence yourself is to dim your resonance. Your words carry power—speak with intention. This chakra shines in sky blue—pure, honest, and resonant.

6. Third Eye (Ajna) – "I See. I Know." The inner vision. Beyond sight—this is the realm of insight. Here lies intuition, foresight, and soul wisdom. When open, you see clearly, beyond illusion. Its color is **indigo**—deep, wise, mysterious.

7. Crown (Sahasrara) – "I Remember. I Am Divine." The thousand-petaled lotus at the top of your head. Your direct connection to Source. Not a belief, but a knowing—that you are a soul wrapped in light, a spark of the Infinite, always connected, always one. This chakra vibrates in violet or pure white—celestial, luminous, timeless.

These centers are not just energy points. They are vibrational thresholds—portals of transformation.

When one is blocked, your signal dims. When aligned, you become a clear transmitter of truth, love, purpose, and power.

Each thought you think, each emotion you feel, each choice you make tunes this internal symphony. You are not separate from your chakras— You are their keeper, their tuner, their instrument.

Your body is a sacred sound chamber. Your breath is the bow. Your soul is the song.

And the chakra system? It is your inner tuning fork, Designed to help you remember that wholeness was never lost— only waiting to be awakened, one note, one breath, one vibration at a time.

EMOTION: THE ENERGY IN MOTION

You've felt it. The heaviness of grief is like a stone pressing against your chest. The fire of anger radiates from your core like a furnace ready to erupt. The flutter of joy—sudden, luminous, like light bursting through your skin.

These are not fleeting moods or inconvenient waves. They are frequencies. Sacred data. Living vibrations are designed to move you.

Emotion is energy in motion. It is your body's sacred language—transmitting truth before words can catch up. It flows through your nervous system, your cells, your electromagnetic field. It speaks not to punish you, but to guide you. To tune you. To free you.

When you suppress emotion—when you stuff it down, dismiss it, deny it— you do not silence it. You bury it alive. And in doing so, you distort your internal code. Your energy contracts. Your frequency falters. Your body holds the burden.

But when you feel, when you honor the wave without judgment, when you breathe through it and give it safe passage— you return to resonance. You return to yourself.

Emotion is not your enemy. It is not a flaw. It is not weakness. It is a sacred current of truth, trying to move you. Trying to recalibrate your field. Trying to guide you back to the original signal of your soul.

Grief says, *"Something mattered."* Anger says, *"A boundary has been crossed."* Fear says, *"There is uncertainty—stay aware."* Joy says, *"This is alignment. More, please."* Every emotion is a message. A compass. A vibration with purpose.

You don't need to analyze it. You don't need to fix it. You need to listen. To let it move.

Emotion is a sacred guest— not meant to take up permanent residence, but to pass through, leave its wisdom, and go.

So let it come. Let it speak. Let it teach. Let it leave.

Your job is not to be unmoved. Your job is to be *in motion*— with your breath, your truth, and your heart wide open.

Because when you allow your emotions to flow freely, you become the river again. Clear. Alive. Whole.

And in that motion, you remember: You are not broken. You are becoming.

THOUGHT: THE ARCHITECT OF REALITY

Every thought you think is not silent. It speaks—electrically, energetically, vibrationally.

Each thought sends a signal, A spark in the brain, An impulse through the body, A code into the field.

One thought may pass like a breeze— But repeated thoughts? They become patterns. Patterns become programming. And programming becomes the energetic architecture of your reality.

You build your life from the inside out— not with bricks or boards, but with beliefs.

If you think again and again, *"I am not enough," "I always get left behind," "Nothing ever works out for me,"* you are sending those commands into your biology, into your energy field, into the quantum blueprint from which reality is drawn.

And the universe, ever attuned to resonance, echoes back what you emit— not as punishment, but as partnership. It is always responding to your frequency, not your words alone.

But here is the miracle: You can rewrite the code.

When you shift your thought to— *"I am remembering my power," "I am whole," "I am aligned with divine truth,"* —you begin to shift the entire symphony of your being.

Your breath changes. Your posture softens. Your emotions rise to meet the new vibration. Your outer world begins to recalibrate.

This is not self-help. This is sacred technology.

The thoughts you think are not just inner noise. They are vibrational instructions. They are pulses of energy broadcast into the quantum field, either reinforcing illusion or realigning you with truth.

You are not a victim of your mind. You are the programmer of your frequency. The conscious creator of your tone. The one who decides what reality you resonate with.

So ask yourself gently: What am I thinking? What am I creating with those thoughts? And what truth am I ready to claim?

Because once you change the architect, the architecture begins to change.

Awakening Dormant Codes *A Sacred Remembering*

So how do you begin to unlock the sacred code that lives within you— the one etched in light, wrapped in silence, and waiting beneath your skin?

You do not need to push. You do not need to strive, force, or prove yourself worthy. The divine code was never locked because of your failure— only hidden, gently, until you were ready to see with new eyes.

And now you are ready. Not because of what you've done— But because of what you are willing to feel. Willing to remember. Willing to become.

Your codes awaken not through control, but through communion.

They stir to life through soft devotion— through breath, sound, stillness, and love.

Let these sacred tools guide your return:

- **Sound** Vibration is the original key. When you chant sacred tones—like *OM*, or the ancient Solfeggio Frequencies— you are not just making sound. You are sending light into form. You are activating inner structures, gently tuning the energetic geometry of your body. Each tone reawakens a frequency your cells remember.
  Let the sound arise from your center, not your throat. Let it vibrate you open.
- **Breath** Breath is the bridge between the seen and unseen. Every deep, rhythmic inhale is an invitation. Every exhale, a release. When you breathe consciously, you awaken memory stored not in your mind, but in your cells. The body begins to soften. The nervous system relaxes. And the dormant becomes active.
  With each breath, you are saying to the universe: *"I am here. I am open. I remember."*
- **Affirmation** Words are not just thoughts spoken aloud— They are vibrational codes. Each time you speak loving language over yourself, you rewrite your emotional script. You give

your subconscious permission to evolve. You become the voice you've been waiting for.

Say it often. Say it gently. Even if you don't fully believe it yet— the repetition is the resonance that builds your becoming.

- **Stillness** In the space between sound and breath, there is stillness. A quiet so profound, the body itself begins to speak. Stillness is not the absence of life. It is the presence of listening. And in that sacred pause, codes awaken like seeds responding to rain.

  Sit in the silence. It is not empty. It is full of you.

Your system is always listening. Every thought you think, Every word you whisper, Every belief you carry— it is all absorbed, processed, and mirrored by the intelligence of your being.

So be intentional. Be reverent. Speak to yourself like sacred ground. Breathe into yourself like holy space.

You are not just a vessel. You are a sanctuary. A temple of stars and sound. A garden of codes waiting to bloom.

And when you honor yourself— not with perfection, but with presence— the dormant awakens. The unseen responds. And the light in your DNA begins to hum its original song.

You are a sacred space. Treat yourself accordingly. For the divine is not coming to you— It is already within you.

GENTLE WAYS TO AWAKEN YOUR INNER CODES

A Daily Practice of Soft Activation

You don't need to make a grand declaration. You don't need to be perfect or healed or ready in any traditional sense. You only need to show up—softly, honestly, and consistently. This practice is an offering to yourself. A sacred way to tend the light within.

Begin each day with presence, and let the code awaken slowly, like the sun rising from behind the mountains.

1. Sacred Breath (3 minutes)

Close your eyes. Place one hand on your heart and one on your lower belly. Inhale gently through your nose for a count of 4, Hold for 4, Exhale through your mouth for 6.

Repeat this cycle for 3 minutes.

With each inhale, silently say: *"I receive my remembering."* With each exhale: *"I release what is no longer me."*

Let breath be your bridge.

2. Sound Activation (1–2 minutes)

Hum softly or chant a sacred tone—choose *OM*, *AH*, or a Solfeggio frequency. Let the sound rise from your belly. Let it resonate in your chest.

Imagine the sound weaving through your DNA— vibrating old codes awake, aligning you with your true frequency.

Even one minute of intentional sound can change your field.

3. Affirmation Whisper (1–2 minutes)

Speak these (or your own) affirmations aloud or softly to yourself:

- I am remembering who I am.
- I am safe to awaken.

- I am light wrapped in form.
- I honor the codes within me.
- My vibration is my guide.

Say them slowly. Let them enter like blessings, not commands.

4. Stillness and Listening (2–3 minutes)

Sit in silence. No effort. No expectation. Just listen.

Let the space around you be a container. Let the silence hold you. Let the stillness speak. If emotions rise, let them move. If visions or thoughts come, witness them gently.

You are not empty in silence— you are full of light becoming aware of itself.

5. Daily Intention (Write or Whisper)

Before you rise, ask yourself: What frequency do I choose to carry today?

You might write or whisper one word: Grace. Joy. Clarity. Trust. Worthiness. Peace.

Let this be your inner compass for the day ahead.

A BLESSING FOR THE REMEMBERING

May the light within you awaken with gentleness and grace. May your breath be your guide, your voice your tuning fork, and your presence your prayer. May the dormant codes bloom like morning light through sacred windows. You are not lost—you are becoming. And each moment of remembrance is a homecoming.

YOU ARE THE TEMPLE AND THE LIGHT WITHIN IT

You are not broken. You are not lacking. You are not behind, or late, or lost.

You are in the sacred process of remembering— Realigning. Reclaiming. Reawakening.

Every challenge, every question, every ache in your soul has been part of this divine unfolding. Not to punish you, but to pull you inward, back to the place where your light was never dimmed—only hidden.

You are not here to be fixed. You are here to be revealed.

You are the temple, the sanctuary of the sacred, the living altar where Spirit dwells.

You are the pyramid, built in precise harmony with Earth and sky, designed to hold and transmit divine resonance.

You are the crystal, clear and coded, holding ancient memory within your structure—ready to radiate.

You are the transmitter and the signal. The vessel and the vibration. The key and the lock. The student and the remembering.

And as you begin to vibrate at higher frequencies— through thought, through breath, through sound, through love— you awaken what has always been within you.

The dormant codes begin to shimmer. The forgotten wisdom begins to rise. The false identities fall away like old skin, and you stand as you truly are: Whole. Luminous. Divine.

You remember that you are not merely a human wandering through confusion, trying to find your way.

You are a cosmic being, encoded with stars, woven from sacred geometry, infused with the breath of Source.

You are not here to fit in. You are here to light the way.

You are the code. You are the key. You are the awakening that the world has been longing for.

And when you honor the temple of your body, When you speak from the light within, When you live in tune with the frequency of truth— you don't just rise. You *help the world rise with you.*

You are not just carrying the light. You are the light. And you have never been alone.

REFLECTION & ACTIVATION

There comes a moment in every awakening journey when you are invited to turn inward— not to seek more, but to see more.

Not to gather new knowledge, but to remember what has always lived inside you, whispering quietly beneath the noise of the world.

This is that moment. A sacred pause. A soft turning toward your own light.

Let this be more than a journal prompt. Let it be a ritual of reconnection.

Find a quiet space. Breathe deeply. Place your hand over your heart. Close your eyes if you feel called.

Now ask:

What thoughts am I thinking every day that are shaping my vibration? Which thoughts uplift me? Which ones diminish my light? Which ones feel like echoes from someone else's fear—not my truth?

What emotions am I holding that no longer serve my highest frequency? What am I still carrying? What am I afraid to feel? What do I know, deep down, is that it's time to be released with love?

What would it feel like to fully activate the code of who I really am? If I lived from my light—fully, freely— How would I walk? How would I speak? What would I allow into my life? What would I stop hiding from?

Breathe. Listen. Write what comes.

Not from your head— but from your center. From the quiet, golden place within you that already knows the way.

You don't need to force clarity. You don't need to rush the answers. They are not outside of you. They are waiting in your breath. In your stillness. In the silence between heartbeats.

You are not discovering who you are. You are remembering.

Let this be your gentle activation— the moment you say yes to yourself again.

LETTER FROM MY HIGHER SELF

A Sacred Writing Activation

Now that you've asked the deeper questions… Now that you've listened and allowed the answers to stir… It's time to let your Higher Self speak.

This part of you already exists. It is not far away. It is not in the future. It is the truest version of you, already encoded in your soul.

Your Higher Self holds wisdom beyond time, compassion beyond judgment, and vision beyond fear.

In this moment, become the receiver. Let this be a letter written through you— from the version of you who remembers, trusts, and sees clearly.

Instructions:

1. Find a quiet space. Set the intention to receive guidance from your Higher Self.
2. Light a candle, hold a crystal, or place a hand on your heart—whatever feels sacred.
3. Take a few slow, deep breaths.
4. Pick up your pen and write the following at the top of your page:

"A Letter from My Higher Self"

Then begin.

Let the words come through. Don't overthink. Don't edit. Just let it flow.

If you need help getting started, use one of these openings:

- "Dear One, I want you to know…"
- "You have forgotten how powerful you are. Let me remind you…"
- "There is nothing wrong with you. In fact…"
- "I have always been with you, even when…"
- "Here is what I see in you that you haven't yet seen…"

Let the letter be a message of remembrance, healing, and gentle awakening. Let it carry the energy of truth—vibrational, loving, and whole.

TO CLOSE THE PRACTICE:

When your letter is complete, place your hand over your heart and read it aloud. Let every word become a frequency. Let it enter your cells. Let it become your new code.

Then whisper:

"I receive this. I remember. I am ready."

Fold the letter. Keep it near your bed, your altar, your journal. Return to it when you forget who you are.

Because you are not lost. You are not broken. You are becoming—exactly who your soul intended you to be.

CHAPTER FOUR

WORDS AS WANDS

The Spellwork of Speech

You cast spells every day. Not with robes, or candles, or circles of stone— but with every word that escapes your lips, every passing thought you speak aloud, every quiet whisper you aim at yourself when no one else is listening.

Words are not just how we communicate. They are how we create. They are how we sculpt reality from thought, how we encode vibration into form.

A word is a wand. A spell wrapped in sound. And you—yes, you—are the one who holds it.

YOU ARE ALWAYS CASTING

Every *"I am..."* you say is a declaration. Every *"This always happens to me..."* is a summoning. Every sigh of *"I'll never be enough..."* sends a signal through your field, and the universe responds—faithfully, vibrationally, without judgment.

You either bless or bind yourself with the words you allow to pass through your sacred breath.

Your nervous system listens. Your field listens. The quantum listens.

So speak as if the universe is always tuning in— because it is.

THE FIRST SOUND WAS A WORD

"In the beginning was the Word..." This phrase opens the Gospel of John, but its truth echoes through every mystical tradition on Earth.

The **Hindu OM**, the **Egyptian HU**, the **Hebrew RUACH**, the Sufi remembrance, the First Nations' breath of Great Spirit— all speak of an original sound, a sacred frequency that shaped creation into being.

Sound is vibration. Words are concentrated sounds—sacred vibrations wrapped in language. So every word you speak carries a frequency. It either builds or breaks. Lifts or limits. Aligns or disrupts.

And when you speak with emotion, when your words are charged with the electricity of feeling, they become even more powerful. They ripple outward, imprinting your field. They become living intentions.

YOU ARE THE SPELL

Your voice is not just sound. It is alchemy. You can call in, clear out, and re-code your reality.

The question is not if you are casting spells— but which ones.

Are you speaking as your past self? Your wounded self? Your fearful self?

Or are you speaking as your sovereign self? Your divine self? The version of you that remembers their light?

Every time you say, *"I am healing," "I am worthy," "I am aligned,"* you are not pretending. You are activating. You are re-writing the frequency of your life.

Speak as the light. Speak from love. Speak as if your words are painting your future— because they are.

THE SPELLS WE DON'T REALIZE WE'RE CASTING

The Language of Limitation

"I'll never get this right." "That always happens to me." "I'm just not good at that." "I'm too old." "I'm too much." "I'm not enough."

These phrases slip from our lips like smoke— casual, familiar, often unnoticed. We say them in frustration, in jest, in resignation. But here is the truth: They are spells.

Your subconscious does not speak sarcasm. It doesn't filter your words through logic or intention. It doesn't weigh whether you're joking, venting, or repeating something someone else once said.

It hears your tone. It hears your repetition. It hears your emotion.

And then it responds— faithfully, vibrationally, and without question.

Each time you repeat a phrase soaked in self-doubt or limitation, your subconscious begins to align your behavior, your beliefs, and your energy field to match that narrative.

You are not just describing your reality. You are coding it.

We've been taught, *"Watch your actions."* But we must also learn to watch our words— because they are the blueprints beneath our actions. The invisible architecture of our lives.

So begin to notice. Catch the quiet spells you cast when you're tired, discouraged, or trying to be *"realistic."* And gently, lovingly, choose a new tone. Not to be perfect. But to be powerful.

Your words are not habits. They are keys. And you are worthy of using them to unlock the life your soul came here to live.

WORD AUDIT RITUAL

Transforming Your Language, Rewriting Your Frequency

Your words are not just sounds. They are seeds. They carry vibration, intention, memory, and creative power.

This ritual will help you uncover the quiet spells you've been casting—often unconsciously—and gently transform them into words that align with your highest truth.

This is not about guilt. This is about awareness. Awareness is the first step in rewriting your reality.

Step 1: Create Sacred Space

Light a candle, burn incense, or simply touch your heart. Set the intention: *"I am ready to see my words with new eyes. I release old spells and speak from truth."*

Take a few deep breaths to center yourself.

Step 2: The Audit – What Have I Been Saying?

Write down a list of phrases you often say—out loud or in your mind—especially when:

- You're stressed
- You feel inadequate
- You're afraid to try something new
- You talk about yourself, your body, your past, or your abilities

Examples:

- *"I always mess this up."*
- *"Nothing ever works out for me."*
- *"I'm terrible at this."*
- *"That's just how I am."*
- *"I'm not creative."*
- *"It's too late for me."*

Don't judge them. Just notice.

Step 3: The Alchemy – Rewriting the Spell

Next to each limiting phrase, write a new truth—a conscious code that speaks from your empowered self.

Let it feel gentle, but also real.

Examples:

- *"I always mess this up."* → *"I am learning, and I trust the process."*
- *"I'm not creative."* → *"Creativity flows through me in ways that are uniquely mine."*
- *"I'm too old."* → *"My wisdom deepens my magic."*
- *"It's too late for me."* → *"Now is the perfect time to begin."*

Let each new phrase feel like a blessing—one your soul has been waiting to hear.

Step 4: Speak It Into the Field

Choose 3–5 of your new phrases and speak them aloud—slowly, reverently, with your hand on your heart.

Say them as if you're reprogramming your field. Because you are.

Repeat:

"I now release the old spell. I speak from truth. My words are my wand, and I choose to create beauty."

Step 5: Anchor the Change

Write your favorite new phrase on a mirror, a sticky note, or in a journal. Say it every morning. Whisper it every night. Let it become your new internal song.

This is how change begins—not through force, but through frequency.

You are the author. You are the wand. You are the spell.

Speak accordingly.

SACRED SPEECH: THE RETURN OF CONSCIOUS LANGUAGE

Speaking as a Soul in Motion

There is power in every sentence. But when you speak with intention, your words become sacred architecture— building bridges between energy and form, between what is and what can be.

This is not about poetic language or polished grammar. This is about alignment. This is about vibration. This is about remembering that your voice is holy.

Sacred speech isn't about saying the right thing. It's about speaking from the right place— the place within you that remembers who you are, why you're here, and what you are capable of creating with the sound of your soul.

Ask yourself:

- Do my words match the vibration of the life I say I want?
- Do I speak like someone who trusts their vision?
- Do I speak to others as if they are sacred vessels of light?
- Do I speak to myself as if I am a temple, not something broken to be fixed, but something divine to be honored?

Because your words are more than sound. They are signals. They are summonings. They are the way your inner world becomes visible.

Your voice is a tuning fork. It vibrates your energy field. It harmonizes—or distorts—your alignment. It calls in frequencies that match the tone you carry.

Your language is a spell. Each word either weaves your reality closer to your soul's truth— or pulls you deeper into illusion.

And your truth? Your truth is your magic. Your undeniable, unalterable, soul-coded essence.

When you speak from that place— with reverence, with presence, with purpose— you don't just communicate. You create. You bless. You align timelines. You become a living prayer, spoken into the world with every breath.

So let this be the moment you return to your voice. Let this be the day you choose to speak as the light you are. Let every word be a key. Every sentence, a spell. Every breath, a bridge.

You don't need to be loud. You don't need to be perfect.

You just need to be conscious.

Because the universe is listening. And so is your soul.

THE VOICE AND THE BODY: A VIBRATIONAL LOOP

Sound Made Flesh

Your body listens. Not casually, not metaphorically— but intimately, energetically, and immediately.

Every word you speak sends ripples through your nervous system. Every tone, every syllable, every vibration of your voice becomes a message delivered directly to your cells.

Speak with shame, and your body folds in on itself. Your shoulders round. Your chest tightens. Your breath shallows.

But speak with strength— with truth, with presence, with power— and your spine rises like a mountain. Your heart expands. Your eyes begin to shine. Your body remembers.

This is the sacred loop: Your voice is the signal. Your body is the receiver. And the moment you speak, your body begins to mirror what's been spoken.

WORDS BECOME POSTURE, POSTURE BECOMES BELIEF

Your voice doesn't just echo into the air. It echoes into you. The sound you create doesn't stop at your lips— it travels down your spine, through your blood, into your tissues.

This is why affirmations, when hollow or mechanical, often feel ineffective. It's not enough to say *"I am powerful"* if your body is still curled in fear. It's not enough to whisper *"I am worthy"* if your chest is collapsed and your breath is stuck.

To speak with power, you must embody the frequency—even for a breath, even for a flicker.

And when you do—when your voice and your body are in alignment, even for one sacred second— you create a resonance so strong it begins to reprogram the entire system.

The affirmation becomes alive. It moves from thought to breath, from sound to structure, from word to reality.

THE SACRED PARTNERSHIP OF VOICE AND FORM

Your voice and your body are not separate. They are sacred partners—one carries the message, the other becomes the mirror.

When you speak with reverence, your body begins to unfold like a flower in sunlight. When you speak with clarity, your energy organizes itself to match that clarity. When you speak from love, your cells begin to remember what that feels like.

You are not just speaking words. You are sending instructions to your system. You are shaping the temple from the inside out.

So the next time you say, *"I am grounded." "I am enough." "I am open to receive."* Let your body rise to meet it.

Let your spine straighten. Let your breath deepen. Let your chest soften. Let your eyes reflect your soul's knowing.

Even if the voice shakes. Even if it feels unfamiliar. Even if you're not sure you believe it yet.

Because your body will believe it first. And then, it will help you become it.

NAMING IS CLAIMING

The Sacred Art of Speaking into Form

There is profound spiritual power in naming. To name something is to pull it from the unseen into the seen. From the formless into form. From potential into presence.

When you name your desire—clearly, lovingly, unapologetically—you claim your sacred role as a co-creator. You say to the universe: *"This is what I choose to bring into being."*

When you name your fear—not with judgment, but with compassion— you disarm its shadow. You call it out of hiding. And what was once overpowering becomes manageable, movable, transformable.

When you name your truth—boldly, even trembling—you invite freedom. You open a door. You give your inner world permission to live outwardly.

This is not just self-expression. This is spiritual architecture.

Because words are not decorations. They are blueprints. Every time you speak, you shape reality. Every time you name a thing, you ground energy into the field.

Your language is the bridge between soul and structure.

So speak with intention. Speak with awareness. Speak like your words carry light—because they do.

ASK YOURSELF DAILY:

- What am I naming today?
- What am I calling into form with the language I use—about myself, others, my path, my life?
- Am I naming lack… or abundance?
- Fear… or faith?
- Limitation… or expansion?

Let your language become a ritual. Let your naming become a claiming. Let your words pull miracles into motion.

Because when you name something with love, with clarity, with truth— the universe begins to conspire on your behalf. Creation listens. Energy gathers. And form begins to take shape.

REPLACING CURSES WITH BLESSINGS

Turning Self-Sabotage into Sacred Speech

Most people don't realize they are casting curses every day. Not with ritual. Not with malice. Not with intention. But with the quiet, familiar phrases they've learned to repeat to themselves… without question.

"I can't." "I'm not good at this." "I'm always messing things up." "Nothing good ever happens to me." "I'll never change." "I'm too broken." "I'm too late."

These aren't harmless expressions. They are frequencies—spoken spells made of doubt, fear, and inherited pain. They seem casual, even normal. But they are binding codes—shaping your field, instructing your subconscious, and keeping you locked in a version of yourself that no longer matches who you are becoming.

But here is the miracle: Every curse can be reversed.

All it takes is awareness, breath, and the power of sacred replacement. You do not need to shame yourself for what you've spoken. You only need to begin speaking again—this time, with intention.

THE SHIFT FROM CURSE TO BLESSING

When you notice an old, limiting phrase rise to the surface, pause. Breathe. And gently rewrite the spell.

This isn't forced positivity. This is frequency recalibration.

Speak not from denial— but from the deeper truth that lives beneath the wound.

Let your new language become a blessing— A soft, strong declaration of who you are becoming.

Examples:

- *"I can't do this." → "I am learning how to do this with more ease and trust."*
- *"I'm so stupid." → "I am wise, and I'm expanding my awareness every day."*

- *"This is too hard." → "This is challenging me to grow stronger and more resilient."*
- *"I never get it right." → "I'm growing through every experience, and I'm getting clearer every time."*
- *"Nothing ever works out for me." → "Things are unfolding for my highest good—even when I can't yet see it."*

You don't need to believe it perfectly. You just need to speak it lovingly. Because even the tiniest shift in language begins to alter your vibration— and your vibration shapes your reality.

THE PRACTICE OF SACRED REPLACEMENT

1. Listen to yourself with compassion—not criticism. Catch the words that bind you.
2. Pause and breathe. Feel the energy behind what you've just said.
3. Ask gently: What would love say here? What would my higher self declare?
4. Speak the blessing aloud. Let it feel like balm. Let it vibrate through your system.

Do this daily. Do it quietly. Do it like it matters. Because it does.

Every curse you unravel frees your voice. Every blessing you declare reawakens your power.

You are not too far gone. You are not cursed beyond repair. You are simply learning how to speak the language of light again.

So speak like your words are wands. Speak like your soul is listening. Speak like your future depends on it— Because it does.

SPEAK WHAT YOU WANT TO SEE

The universe doesn't just hear your prayers. It hears your patterns.

When you speak what you want to see—consistently, lovingly, truthfully—you magnetize that vibration into your life.

Say:

- *"I trust the timing of my life."*
- *"I am connected to divine intelligence."*
- *"I am whole, even as I evolve."*
- *"I speak from my soul, and my soul speaks back."*

Let your words become invitations, not limitations.

THE BREATH BEHIND THE WORD

Speaking as a Creator, Not a Habit

Remember this: **Words without breath are hollow.** They are sound without soul. They may echo, but they do not resonate.

Because it is not just the word that creates— it is the breath that carries the word into the living universe. Your breath is life force, spirit, the original wind of creation. It is the whisper of the Divine moving through you.

When you speak, you are not merely releasing air from your lungs— You are releasing energy, intention, and vibration.

BREATHE LIFE INTO YOUR WORDS

Before you speak, pause. Feel your breath gather in your body. Let it rise from your belly—not your throat. Let your exhale carry your intention, not just your sound.

Let your tone match your truth. Let your voice become a transmission— not of noise, but of presence.

When you say *"I love you,"* let your breath soften with the vibration of love. When you say *"I am ready,"* let your body rise to match your readiness. When you say *"I am powerful,"* let every cell hear it—let it ring like a bell through your bones.

This is not performance. This is alignment.

YOU ARE NOT JUST SPEAKING TO THE AIR

You are speaking to the field. To the vibrational matrix that responds not to your volume— but to your frequency. Your breath carries the signature of your soul.

When you speak with breath and presence, you are coding reality. You are speaking into the architecture of atoms. You are shaping time. You are impressing intention into the quantum field, where it begins to ripple, respond, and rearrange.

You are not just speaking to be heard. You are speaking to be felt.

To speak without breath is to speak from the mind alone. To speak with breath is to speak from the soul.

SPEAK LIKE YOU KNOW WHAT YOU'RE DOING

Because you do.

Whether you remember it or not, you are a being of vibration, a creator of form, a conductor of breath, sound, and spirit.

So inhale with reverence. Exhale with intention. And let every word become a living bridge between thought and form, between you and the infinite.

BREATH & WORD ALIGNMENT PRACTICE

A Ritual for Speaking with Power and Presence

This is not just breathwork. This is energy work. This is conscious creation with your voice, your body, and your intention—united in rhythm.

When you pair your words with your breath, you charge them. You send them into the field as living frequencies. You don't just say the truth—you become it.

Create Your Sacred Space

Find a quiet place where you can sit or stand comfortably. Close your eyes for a moment. Place one hand on your heart, and one hand on your lower belly.

Take three deep, slow breaths. Inhale through your nose. Exhale gently through your mouth.

With each breath, feel yourself arriving— into your body, your moment, your voice.

The Alignment Cycle (Repeat for 3–5 Rounds)

1. **Inhale (4 counts):** Breathe in through the nose and silently say: *"I receive the truth of who I am."*
2. **Hold (2 counts):** Feel your energy collect. Let the intention root.
3. **Exhale (6 counts):** Release through the mouth and speak aloud:

"I am powerful." "I am aligned." "I am worthy." "I am love." (Choose one or rotate through them as feels right.)

Let your breath carry the word like wind carries a seed.

Let your tone rise from your core, not just your mouth. Speak slowly. Speak fully. Let the vibration echo through your body.

OPTIONAL AFFIRMATIONS TO CYCLE THROUGH

- *"I speak only what serves my highest truth."*
- *"My breath is my bridge between spirit and form."*
- *"My words are sacred and alive."*
- *"I command reality with love, not fear."*
- *"My voice is my wand."*

Repeat this cycle until you feel a shift in your body— a softening, an awakening, a sense of arrival.

SEAL THE PRACTICE

Place both hands over your heart. Whisper:

"I speak from my soul. I breathe with intention. I live in alignment."

Let a final breath rise and fall, and feel the stillness settle in.

You are now speaking from alignment. Let your day reflect that truth.

YOU ARE THE VOICE OF LIGHT

You were never meant to shrink your voice to fit into silence. You were born to vibrate truth, to speak light into form, to sing frequencies that heal.

Every time you speak with love, you lift the world's vibration. Every time you speak with courage, you unlock doors for someone else. Whenever you speak to yourself with tenderness, you repair the sacred web within.

Your words are wands. Your breath is the wind. And your voice is the song the universe has been waiting for.

Use it well. Use it true. Use it now.

REFLECTION & ACTIVATION

Ask yourself: What are the three most common phrases I say to myself? Do they empower me or diminish me? What would I sound like if I spoke only from love, truth, and vision?

Write a new phrase—a sacred spell—that you will begin to say daily. Let it become your new vibration.

INTRODUCTION TO THE AFFIRMATION CARDS

How to Use These Spoken Frequencies to Transform Your Life

Words are not just language. They are frequency. They are energy. They are creations in motion.

These affirmation cards were designed to reconnect you with your creative power—to awaken the sacred spellcaster within. Every word you speak forms a pattern in your energetic field. Every sentence you repeat becomes a thread in the fabric of your reality.

These are not just lovely thoughts. They are vibrational codes—spoken activations that bring your mind, body, and spirit back into harmony with truth.

HOW TO USE THESE CARDS

There's no wrong way to use these affirmations. Your intention is what gives them life. Here are some inspired ways to invite them into your daily practice:

Morning Activation

- Choose one affirmation each morning.
- Speak it aloud three times, slowly and clearly.
- Breathe between each repetition. Feel it settle in your body.

Evening Reflection

- Reflect on your day: What thoughts or words challenged your peace?
- Choose an affirmation that brings healing or realignment.
- Whisper it gently to yourself before rest.

Journaling Companion

- Write an affirmation at the top of your journal entry.
- Explore how it makes you feel, what it brings up, or what it inspires.

Sound Practice

- Record yourself reading a selection of affirmations.
- Play it as part of your meditation or morning walk.
- Let your voice become your medicine.

Ritual or Prayer

- Light a candle. Hold the card or phrase in your hands.
- Speak it into the flame, the air, the earth, or the stars.
- Send it out like a prayer wrapped in frequency.

On-the-Go Reminder

- Print or write one down and keep it in your pocket or bag.
- Let it be a touchstone when you must return to your center during the day.

Let the Cards Choose You

If you feel called, let your intuition guide you:

- Shuffle the deck (or scan the page with closed eyes).
- Ask: What do I need to hear today?
- Choose the one that speaks to your spirit.
- Trust that it's precisely the frequency your field needs.

YOU ARE THE SPELL

Remember, it is not just the words that hold the power— you. Your belief. Your breath. Your willingness to shift.

These cards are mirrors of your divine self. They are reminders, invitations, and keys.

Speak them not as a hope but as a knowing. Speak them not with fear but with faith. Speak them not once—but again and again until your body believes it, until your life reflects it.

You are not waiting for magic. You are the magic. Let your words remember that.

AFFIRMATION CARDS: WORDS THAT HEAL, WORDS THAT ACTIVATE

"Affirmations are not wishful thinking. They are intentional codes, vibrating in rhythm with who you are becoming." —Tina Ketch

These affirmations are designed to be spoken daily—morning, evening, or whenever your energy needs realignment. Speak them out loud, whisper them, write them, carry them, and let them shape your vibration.

Sacred Voice Series

- *"My words are sacred. My voice is power."*
- *"Everything I speak returns to me multiplied. I choose love."*
- *"I am safe to speak my truth with clarity and grace."*
- *"My voice is the sound of my soul."*
- *"I no longer echo my fear—I now declare my destiny."*
- *"What I speak, I shape."*

- *"I release the language of limitation. I speak light."*

Healing & Reprogramming Series

- *"I speak to myself with compassion and reverence."*
- *"I forgive the words I once believed that were never mine to carry."*
- *"Every word I speak heals a part of me."*
- *"I replace inner criticism with sacred affirmation."*
- *"I unlearn the lies and relearn the truth of who I am."*

Manifestation Series

- *"I speak what I wish to see, and the universe listens."*
- *"My words are aligned with divine timing."*
- *"I speak in resonance with the life I am calling forth."*
- *"I am in harmony with all that is unfolding for my highest good."*
- *"I use my voice to open portals of possibility."*

Chakra Alignment Series

- **Throat Chakra:** *"I express myself with clarity and authenticity."*
- **Heart Chakra:** *"My words flow from love."*
- **Solar Plexus:** *"I trust in the power of my voice."*
- **Root Chakra:** *"I speak from a grounded place of truth."*
- **Crown Chakra:** *"Divine wisdom flows through my words."*

Daily Devotional Series (One Per Day)

- **Monday:** *"Today, I speak peace into every space I enter."*
- **Tuesday:** *"Today, I choose words that nourish and uplift."*
- **Wednesday:** *"Today, I rewrite my inner dialogue in love."*
- **Thursday:** *"Today, I speak in alignment with my purpose."*
- **Friday:** *"Today, I declare abundance over my life."*
- **Saturday:** *"Today, my voice creates clarity and connection."*

- **Sunday:** *"Today, I bless myself and others with sacred words."*

How to Use These Affirmations:

- Read one aloud each day as your morning activation.
- Write them in your journal to deepen the connection.
- Record them in your own voice and play them during meditation.
- Carry a favorite one in your pocket or place it on your altar.
- Create your own. Speak what your soul wants to hear.

AFFIRMATION CARDS – EXPANSION SET

"Every affirmation is a sacred breath, shaping the world I walk into." —Tina Ketch

Divine Identity Series

- *"I am not becoming—I remember who I've always been."*
- *"I am a frequency of light in human form."*
- *"I walk as wisdom, wrapped in skin."*
- *"My essence is ancient, my presence is divine."*
- *"I am not small. I am stardust shaped by love."*

Celestial Connection Series

- *"I move with the rhythm of the stars."*
- *"The moon is my mirror, and I trust its timing."*
- *"I am aligned with the cosmic intelligence that created galaxies."*
- *"Every breath I take harmonizes with the heartbeat of the universe."*
- *"I belong to the sky, the sea, and the sacred space between."*

Empowerment & Protection Series

- *"I no longer shrink to fit what I've outgrown."*
- *"My energy is sovereign. My spirit is unshakable."*
- *"I am a force of light in a world remembering how to shine."*
- *"I choose boundaries that honor my soul's vibration."*
- *"I protect my frequency with grace and power."*

Grounding & Centering Series

- *"I am rooted in truth and open to miracles."*
- *"The Earth supports me. I am safe here."*
- *"I return to myself with every breath I take."*
- *"Even in uncertainty, I am steady."*
- *"Stillness is sacred. I do not rush divine timing."*

Heart-Centered Series

- *"I love from overflow, not depletion."*
- *"My heart is my compass, and I trust its wisdom."*
- *"I release the fear of being too much or not enough."*
- *"I am always worthy of love, peace, and belonging."*
- *"I forgive myself and return to love."*

Quantum Creation Series

- *"My vibration is my message to the universe."*
- *"I speak, I feel, I imagine—and reality responds."*
- *"I live in alignment with what I desire, not what I fear."*
- *"Everything I seek is already seeking me."*
- *"I am in flow with miracles, magic, and manifestation."*

Bonus Activation Cards

- *"Every step I take is guided. Every breath I take is sacred."*
- *"I honor the frequency of my now, while dreaming boldly into my next."*
- *"When I speak truth, I dissolve illusion."*

- *"My frequency is medicine—for myself and for the world."*
- *"I am not waiting—I am awakening."*

CHAPTER FIVE

EMOTIONS AS ALCHEMY

The Sacred Fire Within

Emotion is not a weakness. It is not chaos to be avoided or a flaw to be hidden. Emotion is a force. A sacred element. A divine technology is woven into your human design.

You were not born to suppress your feelings. You were born to feel them, to listen to them, to alchemize them.

Emotion is not the enemy. It is the initiation.

It is your soul's language— a vibrational current that rises through the body not to harm you, but to wake you up.

Every emotion is a messenger. A carrier of light. A sacred code wrapped in energy, asking only to be acknowledged, honored, and felt.

WHEN YOU FEEL, YOU HEAL

Grief is not a void. It is proof that something matters. Anger is not destruction. It is a boundary calling for restoration. Fear is not a flaw. It is a guardian asking you to pause and pay attention. Joy is not fleeting. It is a remembrance of your original frequency.

Emotions are not problems. They are portals.

Each time you feel one fully—without judgment, without rushing away—you step into the fire of transmutation. You enter the realm of emotional alchemy, where energy becomes wisdom, and pain becomes power.

SUPPRESSION DISTORTS. HONOR ALIGNS.

When you ignore your emotions— when you dismiss, bypass, or bury them— you don't silence them. You simply drive them deeper into your field, where they twist, tighten, and eventually disrupt your frequency.

But when you turn toward your emotions— with presence, breath, and compassion— you begin to clear the static. You become more magnetic, more truthful, more whole.

Emotional mastery isn't about feeling less. It's about feeling more intentionally.

It's about becoming the alchemist of your own inner fire.

So the next time a wave rises, don't rush to silence it. Don't apologize for it. Don't exile it from your temple.

Instead— Breathe. Feel. Listen.

And then, like a sacred flame, let it burn away what no longer serves.

What's left behind will not be brokenness. It will be true. It will be light. It will be you—more aligned, more powerful, more free.

WHAT IS ALCHEMY?

The Sacred Science of Soul Transformation

Alchemy is the ancient, mystical art of transformation— the process of transmuting base matter into something luminous, refined, and holy.

In the material world, it was the pursuit of turning lead into gold. But in the spiritual world, true alchemy is not about gold. It is about elevation. It is about turning heaviness into light, density into clarity, suffering into wisdom. It is the sacred process of returning to truth.

Alchemy begins where pain meets presence. It is the moment you stop running from what hurts, and instead turn toward it—with breath, with compassion, with fire in your eyes that says, *"I will make something beautiful from this."*

Emotional Alchemy: The Sacred Fire Within

Emotional alchemy is not metaphor. It is not self-help wrapped in poetry. It is energetic truth.

It is the soul's innate ability to take raw, overwhelming emotion and transmute it into strength, clarity, wisdom, and grace.

It is the art of:

- Turning fear into courage
- Turning grief into depth and wisdom
- Turning anger into protection and empowerment
- Turning shame into compassion and truth
- Turning heartbreak into open-heartedness

This isn't symbolic. It is vibrational. Every emotion is energy. And energy, when allowed to move, transforms.

EMOTION IS ENERGY IN MOTION

The word emotion comes from the Latin emovere— which means *"to move out"* or *"to stir from within."*

Emotion is energy in motion. When it flows, it clears. When it's held back, it stores.

Stored emotions become density in the body. They show up as fatigue, tension, illness, disconnection, numbness, anxiety, or chronic fatigue. Not because the emotion is bad— but because it was never allowed to complete its sacred cycle.

But here's the miracle: You do not need to fear your emotions. You were designed to feel. You were designed to *move* emotion—not to be destroyed by it, but to be refined through it.

Emotions are not your enemy. They are your inner fire, your sacred water, your breath of change.

PAIN IS NOT THE PROBLEM—RESISTANCE IS

We have been taught to fear our feelings. To silence grief. To control anger. To ignore fear. To hide sadness. To *"be strong"* and hold it all in— even as our hearts are screaming for release.

But hear this truth: Pain does not create suffering. Resistance does.

Suffering is not the result of feeling too much— it's the result of not letting yourself feel at all.

Suppression is not strength. It is silence in the face of the sacred. It is spiritual amnesia.

True strength is not in suppression—it is in presence. It is in the courage to sit with what rises, to breathe through it, to say, *"This, too, belongs. And I am willing to feel it."*

When you allow emotion to move through you, you allow your soul to heal itself. You become the alchemist. You become the flame.

THE SACRED MAP OF EMOTION

Every emotion carries a frequency. Every emotion holds a message. None are wrong. None are shameful. All are sacred messengers calling you home to yourself.

- **Grief** teaches release. It clears space for what is new to enter.
- **Anger** reveals boundaries. It burns through falsehood to protect your truth.
- **Fear** asks for safety. It invites you to cultivate presence, awareness, and trust.
- **Shame** signals misalignment with your soul's truth. It asks for gentle, radical self-forgiveness.
- **Sadness** softens your edges. It opens the heart and waters the seeds of compassion.
- **Joy** is a signal of alignment. It expands your field and connects you to your soul's vibration.
- **Love** dissolves separation. It is the highest frequency, the original tone of your being.

No emotion is here to punish you. Each one is here to guide you, to open you, to transform you.

They are not obstacles. They are initiations.

And when you stop seeing emotions as enemies, and start honoring them as alchemical ingredients, you reclaim your power as the one who turns heaviness into light.

FEEL TO HEAL: THE THREE-STEP ALCHEMY PROCESS

A Sacred Practice of Transformation

Emotional alchemy begins not with doing, but with being— with allowing, witnessing, and honoring what rises within you.

You cannot transform what you will not feel. And you cannot heal what you refuse to see.

This is the sacred work. This is how you turn pain into power, emotion into clarity, wounds into wisdom.

Let these three steps become your ritual of return— a gentle, powerful process for transmuting emotional energy into light.

1. Feel It Fully

Pause. Close your eyes. Breathe deeply into your body.

Let the emotion rise—without resistance, without judgment. Not to fix it. Not to label it. Not to run from it.

Ask gently: *"What am I truly feeling beneath this thought, this reaction, this tightness in my chest?"*

And then... just feel. Feel without the need to understand. Feel without the need to solve. Let it wash over you like a wave you were born to ride.

This is not weakness. This is presence. This is power.

2. Name It with Compassion

What you name, you tame. What you name, you claim. And what you claim, you begin to transform.

Speak it softly or write it down:

"I feel sadness." "I feel anger." "I feel fear, shame, grief."

Say it as if you're telling a sacred truth—because you are.

Naming your emotion brings it out of the shadows and into the light. It creates space between *you* and the feeling. It reminds your nervous system: *"I am safe to feel. I am safe to heal."*

Let the name be your doorway to deeper clarity.

3. Move It Through

Emotion is not meant to be stored. It is meant to move.

Let your body become the vessel of release: Cry. Breathe. Shake. Sway. Dance. Write. Scream into a pillow. Sing a sound you've never sung before.

Lay the weight at the feet of the Divine.

You do not need to know how it will leave— only that it wants to go. That it needs to go. That it was never meant to stay stuck inside of you.

Let it rise. Let it speak. Let it move.

This is sacred work. This is emotional alchemy.

EMOTIONAL ALCHEMY IS SPIRITUAL MATURITY

Spiritual maturity is not about avoiding emotion. It's not about never getting triggered or always being calm.

It's about responding with awareness instead of reacting with resistance. It's about saying,

"This emotion is rising for a reason. I choose to stay present."

This is courage. This is self-love in motion. This is the moment you reclaim a part of yourself you once pushed away.

Every time you meet yourself with presence instead of judgment, you restore order to your inner temple. You bring coherence back to your system. You align your frequency with truth.

This is the real work of the soul. This is what healing looks like in motion. This is what it means to feel to heal.

Sound, Scent & Movement in Emotional Healing

Because emotions are made of energy, they respond beautifully to vibrational tools:

- **Sound**: Humming, chanting, singing, or listening to Solfeggio Frequencies can vibrate stuck emotion free. Let your voice become a tuning fork for release.
- **Scent**: Essential oils like lavender (soothing), frankincense (cleansing), rose (heart-opening), or sandalwood (grounding) calm the nervous system and open emotional pathways.
- **Movement**: Five minutes of conscious movement—shaking, swaying, stretching, walking barefoot—can shift your entire energetic field.

Healing doesn't always look like stillness. Sometimes it looks like motion, sound, surrender. Sometimes it looks like allowing the wave to move through you completely.

Let your tools become your allies. Let your body become your guide.

YOUR EMOTIONS ARE YOUR TEACHERS

You were not born to bypass, bury, or silence your emotions. You were born to partner with them. To walk alongside them like old friends bearing gifts you didn't know you needed.

When you make space for your sadness, you make room for peace. When you allow your anger, you awaken your boundaries. When you sit with your fear, you discover your courage. When you embrace your grief, you find your gratitude.

You are not broken. You are breaking open.

You are not weak. You are becoming whole.

Your emotions are not against you. They are sacred. And so are you.

AFFIRMATIONS FOR EMOTIONAL ALCHEMY

Repeat these aloud, with breath and presence:

- *"I honor all of my emotions as sacred signals."*
- *"I allow myself to feel deeply and heal gently."*
- *"There is wisdom in every wave of emotion I experience."*
- *"I transform pain into power with love and presence."*
- *"I trust the process of emotional release and renewal."*
- *"My feelings are not flaws. They are frequencies of truth."*
- *"As I feel, I heal. As I heal, I rise."*

REFLECTION & ACTIVATION

A Sacred Dialogue With the Fire Within

There comes a moment in every healing journey when you must pause— not to analyze, not to escape, but to listen.

To turn inward with reverence. To ask the questions that open the gates. To become still enough to hear what your soul has been trying to say all along.

This is that moment. A holy threshold. A quiet encounter between who you've been and who you are becoming.

Let your reflection become a ritual. Let your presence become your healer.

Take a breath. Take your time. And gently ask:

What emotions do I resist the most?

Which feeling do I avoid at all costs? Is it sadness? Anger? Fear? Shame? What happens in my body when it begins to rise? Where do I run—into distraction, into numbing, into silence?

What am I afraid will happen if I let myself feel it all the way through?

What might this emotion be trying to teach me?

If this feeling were a messenger instead of a mistake— what would it be saying?

- Is grief inviting me to let go of something I've outgrown?
- Is anger asking me to protect what matters?
- Is fear calling me to slow down and look deeper?
- Is shame trying to point me back to my own truth?

What sacred insight might be hidden within this pain?

What would it look like to honor this emotion instead of fear it?

If I stopped resisting and started allowing—what would shift?

What would it look like to sit beside this feeling and say,

"I see you. You belong. You are safe to move through me now."

How would my body respond if I trusted the wave instead of bracing against it?

LET YOUR JOURNAL BECOME A SACRED CONTAINER

Write it down. Not to solve it. Not to fix it. But to give your emotions a voice. To open a space where your pain is not judged—but heard. Where your feelings are not feared—but felt.

Let your words hold space for what your heart has carried in silence.

LET YOUR BREATH BECOME YOUR COMPASS

Return to your breath, again and again. When emotion rises, do not abandon yourself. Inhale presence. Exhale permission.

With every breath, remind your body: *"I am safe. I am here. I can feel this."*

Your breath is not just air. It is your anchor, your guide, your bridge back to wholeness.

LET YOUR PRESENCE BECOME YOUR HEALER

Healing is not something you force. It is something you allow.

And the greatest healing happens when you are fully present with what is— without running, fixing, or apologizing for it.

Presence is where the alchemy begins.

Because inside of you is a sacred fire— a flame that has always known how to transform pain into power, fear into focus, grief into grace.

This fire was never here to burn you. It is here to burn away what no longer serves. It is here to illuminate what you forgot you were made of.

It is here to refine you into gold.

So sit with the heat. Trust the flame. Write the truth. Let your emotions rise, move, and release.

Because every time you do— you come home to yourself again.

CHAPTER SIX

THE PYRAMID WITHIN

You are a pyramid. Not just metaphorically—energetically, vibrationally, cosmically. Within you is a sacred structure designed for ascension, alignment, and divine connection.

The ancients did not build pyramids as tombs. They built them as resonant temples—living geometries that could amplify energy, preserve knowledge, and lift the soul.

But here's the truth that has been forgotten: You don't have to visit Egypt to enter a pyramid. Because the most incredible pyramid you'll ever enter is within you.

SACRED GEOMETRY: FORM THAT HOLDS FREQUENCY

A pyramid is one of the most potent energetic shapes in existence. Its structure follows the principles of sacred geometry, forming a stable base with a rising apex—a physical embodiment of earth meeting spirit.

Why pyramids?

- Because they gather energy at the apex and direct it upward.
- Because they align with celestial bodies and magnify frequencies.
- Because they symbolize the journey from density to light—from the physical to the divine.

In nature, energy follows structure. Whether made of stone or spirit, the pyramid form acts like a tuning fork, amplifying everything within it.

That means your inner pyramid can amplify peace… focus… healing… or whatever intention you place at its center.

YOU ARE BUILT LIKE A PYRAMID

The more you study the pyramid, the more you'll see it reflected in your own being.

- Your body is the base: physical, grounded, foundational.
- Your heart is the center: emotional, intuitive, balancing all above and below.
- Your mind is the apex: focused, imaginative, reaching toward divine awareness.
- Your breath is the bridge between all levels—rising and falling like sacred wind through the structure of your soul.

You are built to rise. You are meant to ascend from survival to sensation, logic to light.

Each level of your being is a chamber—just like the pyramid itself. And within each chamber lies a code, a key, a vibration ready to awaken.

THE INNER CHAMBERS

Let us walk the pyramid within you.

Chamber One: The Foundation (Root/Body)

This is your physical form—your grounding, your stability. The lessons here are trust, safety, presence, and survival. If this level is unstable, the entire structure above begins to wobble.

Mantra: *"I am safe. I am grounded. I belong to the Earth."*

Chamber Two: The Heart (Balance & Compass)

This is your emotional center, the chamber of compassion and coherence. Here, you decide whether to build walls or open doors. This is where love becomes frequency, and forgiveness becomes alchemy.

Mantra: *"I am love. I give and receive in equal measure."*

Chamber Three: The Apex (Vision & Voice)

This is the summit—the inner eye, the channel of divine insight. Here, you connect to the cosmos. You receive downloads. You transmit truth. When this level is activated, your words become sacred, your thoughts become light, and your visions become clear.

Mantra: *"I am light. I speak and live my highest truth."*

Together, these chambers create the inner pyramid—a living temple of energy, form, breath, and soul.

Alignment Through Geometry

When your inner pyramid is in harmony, energy flows upward and downward with ease:

- You feel centered.
- Your decisions feel aligned.
- Your emotions pass cleanly through you.
- You feel connected both to the Earth and to something greater than yourself.

But when your pyramid is out of alignment?

- You feel scattered.
- Your words lack power.

- Your thoughts feel heavy or confused.
- Your foundation (body, home, health) begins to destabilize.

That's when it's time to step back into the temple. To enter the pyramid within.

GUIDED VISUALIZATION: ENTERING THE PYRAMID WITHIN

Take a moment. Breathe deeply. Close your eyes. You are about to step into the sacred geometry of yourself.

Imagine yourself standing before a great pyramid. It is made of light. It hums with ancient resonance. As you step inside, the air feels still, warm, wise.

You enter the first chamber—a space of grounding. Feel your feet connected to the Earth. Hear the quiet beat of your own heart.

You move upward into the second chamber—the heart center. You feel emotion rise—soft, gentle, honest. Perhaps you feel gratitude, sadness. You honor whatever is here.

Then, you reach the apex chamber. A single beam of light streams from above. You breathe it in. You feel clarity, expansion, and vision.

In the center of this chamber is a mirror. You look into it. And you see the most authentic version of yourself. Whole. Vibrating. Awake.

Say to yourself: *"I am the temple. I am the light within it."*

And breathe it all in.

USING THE PYRAMID FOR HEALING AND MANIFESTATION

You can work with your inner pyramid in many ways:

- Meditate inside it during stressful moments.
- Visualize it around you before sleep to protect your energy.
- Imagine yourself at the apex when setting intentions or manifesting.
- Return to its chambers when you need alignment.

Each time you enter, it becomes more real. Each time you visualize it, you strengthen your connection to your sacred architecture.

CREATING A PHYSICAL PYRAMID SPACE (OPTIONAL PRACTICE)

For those who feel called, you can create a small pyramid meditation space in your home:

- Use physical pyramid frames (available online) or imagine one energetically.
- Place objects in each "chamber" that resonate with your body (foundation), heart (center), and vision (apex).
- Sit within it and let it magnify your intention, clarity, and calm.

The pyramid doesn't just focus energy—it clears, charges, and aligns it.

YOU ARE THE GEOMETRY OF LIGHT

You don't need to be perfect. You need to be present.

The pyramid within you doesn't demand control. It asks for coherence—that your thoughts, emotions, body, and soul coexist.

When you live from your inner pyramid:

- You walk taller.
- You speak clearer.
- You feel deeper.
- You rise higher.

And when enough people awaken their inner pyramids, the world begins to change.

Affirmations for the Pyramid Within

- *"I am a living temple of light, structure, and sacred purpose."*
- *"My foundation is strong. My center is open. My mind is clear."*
- *"I rise in resonance with my soul."*
- *"I carry the geometry of healing within me."*
- *"I return to the pyramid within whenever I need clarity, strength, or peace."*
- *"The pyramid within me amplifies love, purpose, and truth."*

Reflection & Activation

Ask yourself: What part of my inner pyramid needs the most care right now? Am I grounded? Am I centered? Am I clear?

Journal what you notice. Then, place one hand on your heart and say:

"I honor the sacred structure within me. I am the pyramid. I am the light."

THE PYRAMID WITHIN: A VISUAL GUIDE

This illustration represents the inner pyramid—a sacred structure that lives within each of us. It is layered into three levels, reflecting the energetic architecture of the soul in human form.

At the pyramid's center stands a stylized human figure, symbolizing divine embodiment. The pyramid's tiers are labeled with the three fundamental energetic centers: **BODY, HEART,** and **MIND**. Each level builds upon the one below, creating a sacred ascent from physical survival to divine awareness.

CHAPTER SEVEN

ZODIAC, NUMBERS, AND DIVINE TIMING

You were not born on just any day. You did not arrive into this life at random. You came through a cosmic portal—chosen not by accident but by alignment.

Before your soul enters your body, it chooses a day, a number, a sign, and a rhythm because the timing of your arrival carries energetic meaning. It reveals your soul's orientation, the lessons you came to learn, the gifts you brought with you, and the cycles that most deeply affect your journey.

The universe speaks in symbols, cycles, and seasons. And your birth is its signature.

The Language of the Cosmos

The sky has always spoken. Before we wrote books or built cities, we looked up. The ancients studied the stars, the planets, the moon's rhythms, and the sun's dance across the horizon—not as superstition but as vibrational language.

Astrology and numerology are not about *"predicting the future."* They are about revealing energetic patterns—the underlying current of your life path.

When used with awareness, these tools become not maps of fate but mirrors of potential. They remind you of who you are, why you're here, and how to move with the current of your divine timing rather than against it.

Zodiac: Your Vibrational Orientation

Your sun sign is the sign the sun was moving through at the moment of your birth. But it's more than personality—it's your core frequency. It reveals the energetic blueprint you came into this world with.

Each zodiac sign carries its own vibration, symbol, ruling planet, element, and spiritual lesson.

Here are just a few glimpses into the vibrational essence of the signs:

- **Aries** – The spark of creation. Action, courage, and initiation.
- **Taurus** – Grounded beauty. Sensory wisdom, stability, and presence.
- **Gemini** – The messenger. Thought, language, duality, and curiosity.
- **Cancer** – The sacred nurturer. Emotions, memory, and soul family.
- **Leo** – The radiant heart. Creativity, confidence, and divine play.
- **Virgo** – The healer. Precision, ritual, and sacred service.
- **Libra** – The harmonizer. Balance, aesthetics, and relational truth.
- **Scorpio** – The Alchemist. Death, rebirth, and profound transformation.
- **Sagittarius** – The seeker. Expansion, belief, and divine freedom.
- **Capricorn** – The master builder. Structure, purpose, and soul work.
- **Aquarius** – The visionary. Innovation, future truth, and awakening.
- **Pisces** – The mystic. Compassion, unity, and the great return to Source.

But beyond your sun sign are layers: your moon sign (emotional nature), rising sign (soul's presentation), and full birth chart. Together, they form the symphony of your soul's signature.

Numbers as Cosmic Codes

Just as signs reveal your vibrational nature, numbers speak to your soul's rhythm.

Every number carries a frequency, a message, and a lesson. In numerology, the day of your birth, your full birthdate, and even the numerical value of your name are keys to understanding your soul contract.

Some examples:

1. – Leadership, independence, beginnings.
2. – Partnership, balance, intuition.
3. – Communication, joy, creativity.
4. – Stability, discipline, foundations.
5. – Change, freedom, movement.
6. – Harmony, service, family.
7. – Wisdom, introspection, spirituality.
8. – Power, manifestation, abundance.
9. – Completion, compassion, legacy.

Your Life Path Number, derived from your full birthdate, is like your soul's operating system. Your Soul Urge Number, calculated from the vowels in your name, reflects your innermost desires. Your Destiny Number (from your full name) reveals your divine mission.

These aren't just calculations. They are codes—reflections of divine timing and soul design.

DIVINE TIMING:
YOU ARE IN RHYTHM WITH THE UNIVERSE

Just like there are seasons in nature, there are seasons in your life.

There are times for action and times for stillness. Times to plant and times to harvest. Times to rise, and times to rest.

When you live in sync with your timing cycles, you begin to move with less resistance. You stop pushing against the tide and start floating with the current.

Some of these divine rhythms include:

- **Personal Years** (numerology): Each year of your life falls under a 1–9 cycle, influencing the focus and energy of that year.
- **Saturn Return** (astrology): A powerful 28–30-year cycle that marks major transitions and initiations.
- **Lunar Cycles**: New moons for intention, full moons for release.
- **Retrogrades**: Times to review, reflect, and refine.

When you understand the timing of your soul, you no longer fear the pause or the pivot. You begin to trust the timing of everything.

Aligning with Your Vibrational Calendar

Imagine waking up not to a to-do list but to a rhythm. Imagine choosing your work, your rest, your healing, your dreams—not by pressure, but by vibration.

To do that, begin to tune into your personal vibrational calendar.

Ask yourself:

- What is my personal year number, and what lesson is it bringing?
- What season am I in emotionally—beginning, building, harvesting, or releasing?
- What moon phase is the Earth reflecting, and how does it feel in my body?
- What is the lesson of my current astrological transits?

You are not separate from the cosmos. You are in conversation with it.

Practical Daily Alignment Practices

To live in divine timing, you don't need to be an astrologer or numerologist. You just need to listen.

Here are simple practices to help you realign each day:

Morning Check-In:

"What is today's vibration asking of me?" Look at the date. Notice the moon phase. Notice how you feel.

Use Your Birth Number:

Repeat your life path number's affirmation in the mirror each day. Example (Life Path 7): *"I walk with wisdom and seek truth."*

Track Your Personal Year:

Keep a yearly journal reflecting on how each cycle unfolds. This helps you recognize patterns and soul growth.

Moon Rituals:

- **New Moon**: Set intentions. Light a candle. Whisper a desire.
- **Full Moon**: Release what no longer serves. Write, burn, and bless it.

You Were Born on Purpose

The moment you were born, the sky told a story. The numbers whispered a message. The energy aligned to open a doorway—just for you.

You are not here by mistake. You are a rhythm in the divine symphony. And when you begin to live in tune with the cosmos, Life begins to respond differently.

Not because the stars control you— But because they resonate with you.

They are mirrors, not masters. Guides, not gods. Reflections of the vibration you came to embody.

Affirmations for Divine Timing

- *"I trust the rhythm of my life."*
- *"I am aligned with divine timing and sacred flow."*
- *"The universe speaks through signs, numbers, and cycles—I am listening."*
- *"I was born on time, for a reason, with a purpose."*
- *"I live in tune with the cosmic song that carries me."*

Reflection & Activation

Ask yourself: What is the energy of the season I am in right now? What has my birthdate always felt like—it carries a vibration. What might it be? Where am I being invited to align more with the flow and less with force?

Write down any signs, numbers, or cycles you've noticed. Your soul already knows. Let this chapter awaken what your body remembers.

CHAPTER EIGHT

THE GRID AND THE LEY LINES

You Are Not Just on the Earth—You Are Part of Her Song

The Earth is not just a planet. She is a sentient being. A breathing, pulsing, spiraling field of consciousness. She is womb and temple, memory and mystery. And like you, she has an energy body.

Just as you are composed of chakras, meridians, and breath— the Earth has her own sacred anatomy: The Grid—a luminous, planetary nervous system. A divine network of energetic pathways flowing across mountains, oceans, deserts, and cities.

These lines are not imagined. They are ancient, etched into the Earth's memory and into your bones.

They are the ley lines— rivers of sacred current. And they are not just beneath your feet. They are within you.

You are not walking on the Earth. You are walking with her. You are not separate. You are synchronized. You are a note in her harmonic field.

WHAT ARE LEY LINES—AND WHY DO THEY MATTER TO YOU?

Ley lines are the energetic highways of the Earth— invisible threads of power that link sacred sites across time and space. They are not random. They are the Earth's meridians, through which energy flows, pulses, and renews.

These lines:

- Travel in straight paths across vast distances
- Connect temples, pyramids, cathedrals, megaliths, stone circles, and natural vortexes
- Intersect at nodes—power points where energy intensifies and consciousness expands
- Often align with celestial patterns, zodiac degrees, and astronomical events

Ancient civilizations knew. They didn't guess where to build. They listened. They felt. They placed structures on ley lines to amplify spiritual connection, healing, and transmission.

You can still feel it today:

- The hush at Stonehenge
- The deep pulse at the Great Pyramid
- The electricity in Sedona
- The ascension pull of Machu Picchu
- The mystic hum beneath Mount Shasta

These are not just sites. They are portals. And they awaken something in you because you are made of the same grid.

THE EARTH'S ENERGY BODY IS A MIRROR OF YOURS

The Earth has chakras, just like you do. These global energy centers pulse with planetary consciousness. And just like the chakras in your body, they hold specific frequencies and soul lessons for humanity.

Chakra	Location	Theme
Root	Mount Shasta (California, USA)	Grounding, awakening, ancestral life force

Chakra	Location	Theme
Sacral	Lake Titicaca (Peru/Bolivia)	Creativity, divine feminine, sensual energy
Solar Plexus	Uluru & Kata Tjuta (Australia)	Sacred power, inner fire, purpose
Heart	Glastonbury & Shaftesbury (UK)	Unity, compassion, divine love
Throat	Great Pyramid of Giza (Egypt)	Truth, sacred speech, vibrational clarity
Third Eye	Mobile (often linked to rotation)	Vision, prophecy, collective insight
Crown	Mount Kailash (Tibet)	Spiritual transcendence, divine remembrance

These energy centers evolve and shift as humanity awakens. And when you connect with these places—physically, energetically, or spiritually—you activate codes within your own energy field. The Earth awakens in you, and you awaken in her.

HOW TO CONNECT WITH THE GRID—WHEREVER YOU ARE

You don't have to travel across the globe to feel the grid. You only need presence, breath, and intention.

1. Feel the Land Beneath You Stand barefoot. Sit on the ground. Breathe into the Earth and ask:

"What do you want me to feel, to know, to remember?"

2. Tune into Sacred Sites Remotely Your consciousness is not limited by location. Visualize a site. Feel yourself standing there. Let your heart reach it—and it will respond.

3. Use Stones, Crystals, or Maps Sacred objects hold vibration. Hold a stone from a place of power. Meditate with a global map. Imagine golden lines connecting all things—and *you* as a living node.

4. Ask Your Body Where to Go Feel drawn to a certain mountain, city, or shore? Your soul may be remembering its role in planetary healing. Even if you never go—ask:

"What does this place activate in me?"

YOU ARE A GRID WALKER

Just as the Earth has ley lines, you have light lines. You are not separate from the planet—you are her reflection. You are a living, breathing point of energy in her field.

Grid walkers are souls who carry the codes of Earth-keeping and light-anchoring. Often, they feel:

- A deep reverence for sacred land
- A calling to be barefoot, to touch trees, to sing to the sky
- A responsibility to bring light where heaviness lingers
- A knowing that their presence affects energy—even in silence

If this speaks to your soul, you are remembering your ancient role.

You are here not just to walk the Earth. You are here to activate her memory through your presence.

THE POWER OF BEING PRESENT ON THE GRID

You don't need to chant or channel or move mountains. You only need to be present.

When you walk with intention, you bring coherence to the land. When you breathe with the trees, you harmonize with nature's rhythm. When you speak blessings into the air, you shift the field.

The Earth hears you. She feels your feet. She echoes your frequency.

Every step you take is a conversation with consciousness.

GRID CONNECTION MEDITATION

Sit or lie on the Earth. Place your hands or spine against the ground.

Close your eyes. Visualize golden lines of light weaving beneath you like a glowing web. Let your body soften. Let your breath deepen.

Whisper:

"I am aligned with the living body of the Earth."

Feel the energy rise through your body. Let it clear, ground, and awaken you. Stay as long as you feel the connection—and know it is real.

SIGNS YOU'RE NEAR A POWER POINT

- Tingling in the body or subtle vibration
- Deep stillness or sudden emotional release
- Light-headedness or shifts in consciousness
- Heightened intuition or vivid dreams afterward

- Feeling *"reset,"* recharged, or more yourself than before

You'll know—not with your mind, but with your soul. Energy speaks in resonance. You only need presence to hear it.

AFFIRMATIONS FOR EARTH CONNECTION & GRID ALIGNMENT

- *"I am connected to the living grid of the Earth."*
- *"My body is a temple that harmonizes with sacred places."*
- *"Each step I take anchors light into the world."*
- *"The Earth speaks, and I am listening."*
- *"I walk with purpose, presence, and planetary remembrance."*

REFLECTION & ACTIVATION

Ask yourself with reverence:

- Where am I being called to ground more deeply?
- Have I ever stood somewhere that felt holy, though I didn't know why?
- What part of the Earth's energy body do I feel most aligned with right now—Root, Heart, Crown?

Then journal what arises. Sketch a map of the places that call to you. Send breath, light, or love to a place in need.

And stand on the Earth—even if only outside your door—and whisper:

"I remember the way. I am the light. I am the grid."

Because you are.

CHAPTER NINE

THE DIVINE MIRROR

Every person you meet is a mirror. Some reflect your light. Some reflect your pain. Some awaken joy, while others stir your shadows. But all of them—every single one—has shown up to reveal something sacred.

Relationships are not just random encounters of personalities and preferences. They are vibrational meetings of souls bound together by resonance, memory, and divine design.

What you see in another, whether beautiful or complex, is an invitation to see yourself more clearly.

This is the Divine Mirror. Learning to see it with clarity and compassion will forever change how you love, forgive, and navigate this world.

LIFE IS REFLECTIVE, NOT REACTIVE

We tend to believe life is happening to us. But in truth, life is happening through us.

Each person you attract carries a message:

- The overly critical boss may reflect your inner judge.
- The compassionate friend may mirror the love you're finally allowing yourself to receive.
- The soulmate who triggers deep healing may be the one who mirrors an unhealed wound you're now ready to transmute.

This isn't about blame. It's about awareness. It's about recognizing that people don't just show you who they are—they often show you who you are becoming, who you've been, or what still needs your loving attention.

VIBRATIONAL ATTRACTION

You don't attract what you want. You attract what you are vibrating.

Your frequency is a living field of energy—a blend of your thoughts, emotions, patterns, and beliefs. And that frequency acts like a signal, drawing in people who resonate with it on some level.

- If you vibrate in fear, you may attract people who amplify it.
- If you vibrate in truth, you'll magnetize others who live in authenticity.
- If you vibrate in healing, even the wounded ones you meet will serve a higher purpose.

Sometimes we attract lessons. Sometimes we attract mirrors of our magnificence. And sometimes, we attract a soul contract.

SOUL CONTRACTS: SACRED AGREEMENTS BEYOND TIME

Before you entered this life, your soul made agreements with other souls. You said: *"I'll meet you in this life to help you grow, heal, awaken, and remember."*

These are not always easy connections. Some contracts are wrapped in love. Others are wrapped in friction. But all are woven in purpose.

Types of soul contracts include:

- The Mirror – Reflects a part of you needing to be seen
- The Teacher – Brings wisdom, even through pain
- The Healer – Guides you through a transformational period

- The Catalyst – Awakens you quickly, often through disruption
- The Companion – Walks beside you in mutual support
- The Twin Flame / Sacred Mirror – Forces you to confront and clear everything that is not truth

You may not always understand these contracts when they appear. But you'll feel them. A sense of déjà vu. An energetic *"pull."* A lesson that lingers long after the moment has passed.

WHAT ARE YOU SEEING IN OTHERS?

The people you meet don't define you, but they can reveal you.

Here's a way to discern what someone is mirroring:

- If someone inspires you, ask: What part of me is being activated by them?
- If someone triggers you, ask: What wound is being touched in me that still needs attention?
- If someone annoys you, ask: What belief or boundary in me is being tested?
- If someone supports you, ask: What frequency am I finally learning to allow?

You don't have to take on others' energy. You only have to observe what's being stirred in yours.

PRACTICING CONSCIOUS REFLECTION

We cannot control how others show up. But we can choose how we respond.

When you move from reaction to reflection, you begin to:

- Detach from blame

- Step into compassion
- Take responsibility for your energy
- Learn faster, love better, and heal deeper

This is the path of emotional maturity and spiritual power.

Try this in a moment of conflict or confusion:

Pause. Breathe. Ask: *"What is this person mirroring back to me?" "Is this a wound... a gift... a pattern... a reminder?"*

Then, respond from awareness—not from reaction.

This small act of presence changes everything.

HEALING THROUGH RELATIONSHIP

Often, the people who hurt us the most are not villains. They are mirrors—showing us where we've abandoned ourselves, still carry wounds, or our power has not yet been reclaimed.

This doesn't mean you have to stay in harmful dynamics. Boundaries are sacred. Discernment is divine.

But even in walking away, you can ask:

"What was this person here to show me?" "What am I reclaiming as I release this?"

You no longer attract the same lesson in another face when you heal the frequency within you.

That is liberation.

YOU ARE A MIRROR TOO

Just as others reflect you, you reflect others. When grounded, loving, and true, your presence becomes healing for everyone around you.

You don't need to fix people. You just need to reflect their light to them until they remember it.

Be the mirror that reminds others who they are. Be the light that helps them find their way home. Be the love that reflects truth—not illusion.

This is the highest service.-

AFFIRMATIONS FOR SACRED RELATIONSHIP

- *"Every relationship is a mirror. I receive the lesson with love."*
- *"I take responsibility for my energy and attract aligned souls."*
- *"I am open to giving and receiving vibrational truth."*
- *"I bless the contracts that come to teach me and the ones that come to heal me."*
- *"I reflect the light in others, and I allow others to reflect mine."*

REFLECTION & ACTIVATION

Ask yourself: Who in my life is reflecting my growth? Who in my life is reflecting an unhealed wound? What relationship has catalyzed my evolution? How can I show up as a conscious mirror for others?

Journal honestly. Bless the mirrors—even the cracked ones. You don't need to fix the past. You only need to see it with new eyes.

And when you do, the mirror becomes a window— Through which your soul can shine

CHAPTER TEN

CONSCIOUS CREATION

You Are the Living Code of the Universe in Motion

You are creating your reality—every moment of every day. Not just with your hands, but with your thoughts, your emotions, your intention, your tone, and your frequency.

Creation is not something outside of you. It is not something you chase, master, or learn from others.

Creation is something you are.

You are the vibration before the form. The spark before the flame. The word before the world.

You are not just a participant in this reality. You are a transmitter, a receiver, a magnet, a mirror, and a master key— when you remember how to align your frequency with divine intent.

This is conscious creation: The art of harmonizing your inner world with your soul's design so that what you attract, what you build, what you speak, and how you live becomes a living reflection of who you were always meant to be.

You are not here to hope. You are here to co-create— with the Field, the Earth, and the Infinite Code encoded in your very being.

THE FIELD IS LISTENING—BECAUSE IT IS YOU

Quantum physics confirms what mystics have always known: There is no separation. There is an invisible field of pure potential, a matrix of energy that connects all life, all thought, all time.

This Field is intelligent. It responds to focus. It responds to frequency. It responds to you—because you are woven into its very structure.

You are not separate from the Universe. You are the Universe experiencing itself through human form. You are the code walking in skin. Every thought you think, every feeling you generate, every belief you carry—creates ripples through the fabric of this Field.

You are the cause and the effect. You are the signal and the receiver. You are the spell and the awakening.

The question is not: Is the Field listening? The question is: What are you saying?

INTENTION + EMOTION + VIBRATION = CREATION

Let's simplify the mystery into motion: Creation is not random. It is rhythmic. It is coded.

1. **Intention** – What do you want? Be clear. Speak it. Declare it.
2. **Emotion** – Can you feel it? Embody it? Let it rise in your body now?
3. **Vibration** – Are your thoughts, words, and actions aligned with that feeling—or resisting it?

When all three harmonize, you create a field of coherence. And in coherence, reality rearranges itself to match your resonance.

If you want love, become love. If you want abundance, vibrate abundance. If you want peace, speak peace, walk peace, think peace.

You cannot plant a seed of fear and expect a harvest of joy.

YOUR MIND IS NOT A STORAGE DEVICE—IT IS A PROJECTOR

Your mind is not here to collect information. It is here to cast vision.

It is a holographic projector— sending out images, beliefs, and expectations into the Field, which then returns them to you as experience.

- When your thoughts dwell on lack, the field organizes to reflect more lack.
- When your thoughts dwell in gratitude, the field amplifies abundance.
- When your thoughts swirl in fear, the field creates barriers to *"protect"* you—while limiting your expansion.

This is not punishment. This is physics.

Your mind doesn't describe your life. It scripts it.

MAGNETISM AND RESISTANCE: CLEARING THE STATIC

Every intention is magnetic. But every unhealed belief creates resistance.

You might say:

"I want love." But beneath that, a wound whispers: *"I am not worthy of being loved."*

You might say:

"I want success." But your energy is laced with: *"Success means I'll lose myself."*

These contradictions become static in the field— mixed signals that blur your creation and delay your manifestation.

To truly create, you must become energetically consistent. You must clear the interference. You must become the clean channel for your desire to flow through.

MANIFESTATION IS NOT CONTROL—IT IS ALIGNMENT

You are not here to chase outcomes or force details. You are here to become the vibration of what you desire and let the field mirror your frequency in divine timing.

Manifestation is not about control. It is about clarity. It is about coherence. It is about receiving with grace what you've already encoded into the field.

Often what arrives is better than what you imagined— because the Field responds not to ego's want but to soul's readiness.

Your task is not to control the *"how."* Your task is to become the *"who"*— the version of yourself who already holds, breathes, and radiates the life you're calling in.

SEEDS OF CREATION: HOW TO PLANT THEM IN THE FIELD

Bring your creation practice into sacred steps:

1. **Clarity** What do you want? Be specific. Be honest. Be bold.------

   "I am calling in partnerships that elevate and support my purpose."

2. **Embodiment** Feel the version of you who already has it. Walk like them. Speak like them. Think like them. Let your being become the magnet.
3. **Emotion** Let gratitude arrive early. Feel it before it comes. Let joy become your invitation, not your reward.
4. **Speak It** Words are living codes. Speak your creation aloud. *"I create with clarity, love, and trust. I receive with openness and grace."*
5. **Release It** Let go. Not in apathy but in trust. Creation doesn't need your control—only your alignment.

INSPIRED ACTION VS. FORCED EFFORT

You are not here to hustle your way to your dream. You are here to flow in rhythm with your soul's knowing.

Inspired action is not frantic—it is fluid. It rises from inner truth, not external pressure.

Ask yourself:

- *"Is this action rooted in fear, or in faith?"*
- *"Am I chasing something, or am I aligning with it?"*

When your actions arise from coherence, the path clears. Time expands. Opportunities unfold.

This is creation through grace. This is a conscious manifestation.

YOU WERE BORN TO CREATE

You were not made in the image of a creator to simply observe. You are not a copy. You are a continuation.

Every time you create— whether through word, art, connection, healing, or intention— you are participating in the original code of creation.

You are not just imagining a better life— you are coding it into form.

You are the spark and the source. The field and the seed. The artist and the breath.

Creation is not something you chase. It is something you allow, anchor, and become.

AFFIRMATIONS FOR CONSCIOUS CREATION

- *"I create with intention, emotion, and aligned vibration."*
- *"My frequency shapes my reality."*
- *"I am a co-creator of my life, my joy, and my path."*
- *"What I embody, I become. What I bless, grows."*
- *"I am the living code of divine creation."*

REFLECTION & ACTIVATION

Ask yourself:

- What do I deeply desire—and am I vibrating in alignment with it?
- What hidden beliefs or emotions might be creating resistance?
- What would it feel like to fully embody the version of me who already lives this reality?

Then—speak your vision. Write your code. Walk as if it is already yours.

Because the field is always listening. And it is ready to respond.

CHAPTER ELEVEN

UNITY, COMPASSION, AND GRACE

There is no *"other."* There is only us—in different forms, faces, and frequencies. And when you remember this truth, your heart begins to open wider than your pain, history, or fear.

Unity is not sameness. It is sacred diversity woven in love. It is the recognition that every soul is a note in the great symphony, And we were never meant to sound the same— Only to play in harmony.

This chapter is an invitation. To walk gently. To speak kindly. To see through the eyes of compassion. And to move through the world with the quiet power of grace.

Because the highest frequency you can ever create with… is love.

WE ARE ALL CONNECTED

You are not a single drop in the ocean. You are the ocean—experiencing itself in one precious form.

Every thought you think, every word you speak, every choice you make ripples outward. The energy you bring into a room becomes part of its field. The way you speak to someone becomes part of their inner dialogue. The way you treat yourself becomes part of what the world learns is possible.

This is not a burden. It is a gift.

Because it means that you can change the world—not by force, but by frequency. Not by changing others, but by becoming the clearest, kindest expression of who you truly are.

COMPASSION: THE BRIDGE BETWEEN SOULS

Compassion is the understanding that everyone is carrying something invisible. It's not about excusing harmful behavior or bypassing truth. It's about meeting each moment with presence rather than punishment.

Compassion says:

"I may not understand your journey, But I will not contribute to your suffering."

"I see your wound, and I choose to stay rooted in love."

"I protect my boundaries, but I never abandon my humanity."

We often think compassion is something we extend outward. But the first person who needs your compassion is you.

When you hold space for your own imperfection, you become more spacious with others. When you stop judging your pain, you stop projecting it. When you offer yourself grace, you teach others how to rise without shame.

GRACE: WALKING IN THE FIELD OF LIGHT

Grace is the soft power of the universe. It doesn't push. It doesn't punish. It simply lifts.

To walk in grace is to walk in presence— Knowing that you are part of something bigger. Trusting that even in moments of pain, something holy is unfolding.

Grace does not mean the absence of struggle. It means the presence of love despite the struggle.

It is the light that breaks through shame. The whisper that says:

"Even now, you are worthy. Even here, you are loved."

You cannot earn grace. You can only allow it.

UNITY IN A DIVIDED WORLD

We are living in a time when separation is loud. Fear speaks in headlines. Anger echoes through social feeds. Division disguises itself as *"rightness."*

But beneath the noise, there is stillness. There is a field where love never leaves. And the invitation of this chapter is to live in that field.

To remember:

- We all want to be seen.
- We all carry wounds.
- We all forget sometimes.
- And we all need someone to hold the light while we find our way back.

Unity is not utopia. It's the daily practice of choosing *we* over *me.* It's the courage to say:

"Even if I don't agree with you, I still see your soul."

And sometimes, it's just choosing not to close your heart— Even when the world tries to convince you that you should.

HEALING THROUGH CONNECTION

You are not here to be perfect. You are here to be present. To love in small moments. To listen when it matters. To ask someone how they're doing—and mean it.

Healing doesn't always resemble rituals, meditations, or deep soul work. Sometimes, it looks like a smile, a gentle word, or the choice to stay instead of shut down.

You are a healing presence. Not because you have no wounds. But because you've chosen to love anyway.

That is the highest form of spiritual mastery.

THE FREQUENCY OF WE

We are not meant to ascend alone. The path is not upward—it is inward and outward at once.

To truly live in alignment with the Infinite Code, you must embody the frequency of We:

- We are all rising.
- We are all learning.
- We are all worthy.
- We are all connected by a thread that cannot be broken.

When you see yourself in others, you begin to live as love in form.

AFFIRMATIONS FOR UNITY, COMPASSION, AND GRACE

- *"I walk with compassion, speak with kindness, and live with grace."*

- *"I see the sacred in others, even when they forget it themselves."*
- *"I offer myself the love I've spent lifetimes seeking."*
- *"I am part of the great We—healing, rising, remembering."*
- *"Even in darkness, I am a light."*

REFLECTION & ACTIVATION

Ask yourself: Where am I being called to soften? How can I offer grace without losing my boundaries? Who in my life is reflecting the need for unity rather than division? What does living as a healing presence look like for me today?

Let these answers rise. Let them be small. Because tiny love, given often, becomes a tidal wave.

And when the tide of love rises, All ships lift.

CHAPTER TWELVE

YOU ARE THE CODE

There is no mystery more incredible than the one you carry inside you. No temple is more sacred than your body. No scripture is more alive than your breath. And no code is more powerful than you.

You are not just learning the Infinite Code. You are the Infinite Code. It lives in your cells. It pulses in your heart. It sings in your voice and shines through your eyes. You are the spark, the song, the seed, and the starlight. You are what you have been searching for.

And now, you are ready to remember.

THE JOURNEY OF THE CODE

This book has not been a set of teachings but a return. A spiral inward. A re-alignment with what your soul has always known.

Let us reflect on where you've traveled:

- You began with the hum of creation, the Story Before the Story.
- You breathed with the universe and remembered the power of your voice.
- You activated the pyramid within, uncovered your inner code, and tuned your emotions as alchemy.
- You aligned with the stars, the numbers, the Earth, the field.
- You saw your relationships not as random but as reflections.
- You stepped into conscious creation, then softened into unity, compassion, and grace.

And now—here—you remember: You were never just a student of the code. You are its expression.

YOU ARE THE LIVING BLUEPRINT

Every cell in your body carries divine intelligence. Every thought you think shapes your field. Every emotion you feel carries encoded information—lessons, direction, healing.

You are not a blank slate. You are a living blueprint—a vibrational design sent into this life at this time, in this body, with this frequency, to activate something specific in the world.

Your soul chose the coordinates. Your heart chose the tone. Your mind was meant to awaken slowly— And now, here you are, beginning to see it all.

You are not behind. You are not late. You are exactly on time.

The Infinite Code was never something to be learned from outside. It was always something to be unlocked from within.

THE FRACTAL TRUTH: AS WITHIN, SO WITHOUT

You are not just a soul in a body. You are a microcosm of the macrocosm—a universe walking around in human form.

- Your brain mirrors the structure of the galaxy.
- Your heartbeat matches Earth's resonance.
- Your breath reflects the rhythm of the ocean.
- Your dreams echo the imagination of creation itself.

When you trust your inner world, the outer world begins to mirror your clarity. When you heal your thoughts, you change your energy. When you change your energy, you change your field. And when you change your field—you change the world.

This is not a poetic metaphor. This is vibrational truth.

You are the code… and the coder.

ACTIVATION: LIVING THE CODE

So, what does it mean to live as the Infinite Code?

It means waking up each day and asking:

"What frequency am I choosing today?" "Is this thought, word, or action aligned with my highest self?" "Where can I create beauty, even in small ways?"

To live as the code is to live with:

- **Clarity**: Knowing what you are vibrating
- **Compassion**: Extending grace to yourself and others
- **Creativity**: Realizing you are always creating something
- **Consciousness**: Making choices from presence, not programming
- **Courage**: Choosing to live in alignment, even when it's hard

You do not need to be perfect. You only need to be present.

THE ROLE OF THE REMEMBERED

When you remember who you are, you become a light for others still in the fog.

You do not have to teach them. You do not have to convince them. You must only become what you are—entirely, unapologetically, truthfully.

Your vibration does more than your words. Your presence speaks louder than any doctrine. Your coherence creates ripples that alter timelines.

This is how the world changes—not from the top down, but from the inside out. One awakened human at a time. One living code at a time.

YOU ARE THE THRESHOLD

You are standing at the edge of something vast. A new chapter of your soul's evolution. A timeline where you no longer wait to be chosen—because you remember you already are.

You were encoded with everything you need:

- The light to illuminate the darkness
- The wisdom to navigate the challenge
- The love to dissolve fear
- The presence to activate grace

You are the threshold between what was and what can be.

You are the echo of the stars. The breadth of the field. The voice of remembrance.

You are the Infinite Code.

And you are ready.

INTEGRATION PRACTICE: DAILY CODE ALIGNMENT

Each morning, speak this into your field:

"I remember. I am the code. I align with clarity. I create with love. I walk with grace. I activate the light. I am here now on purpose. And I choose to live fully encoded in truth."

Then pause. Breathe. Step into your day from that space. And return to this whenever you forget.

FINAL AFFIRMATIONS

- *"I am the Infinite Code in motion."*
- *"I trust the design of my soul."*
- *"Every breath I take awakens another layer of my light."*
- *"My presence is an activation for the world."*
- *"I choose to live fully, love boldly, and rise endlessly."*
- *"I am no longer searching. I have arrived."*

THE CODE IS NOW YOURS

This book is not ending. It is only beginning.

Because now, the code lives in your hands. In your choices. In your art, your love, your breath, your legacy.

Let it live. Let it grow. Let it light up the lives of everyone you touch.

And remember:

You were never just part of the story. You were the spark that wrote it. You are the Infinite Code.

And the world has been waiting for you.

CHAPTER THIRTEEN

ANCESTRAL CODES AND SOUL MEMORY

You carry stories in your bones. You breathe with lungs shaped by lineages. You dream with a mind made of memories older than your lifetime. And you walk with a soul that has lived more lives than the world has pages.

You are not just a singular being. You are the living convergence of ancestors, archetypes, and ancient wisdom.

Within you are ancestral codes—emotional patterns, gifts, memories, strengths, and wounds passed to you through blood, vibration, and soul agreement.

And within you, too, is soul memory—the remembrance of lifetimes, realms, and frequencies far beyond this current incarnation.

To unlock your power, you must not only look forward— You must turn inward and backward to face the river behind you. Because healing is not just about your life. It is about your line.

WHAT ARE ANCESTRAL CODES?

Ancestral codes are energetic imprints passed down through generations. These are not just genetic traits. They are vibrational patterns:

- Emotional responses
- Beliefs about love, safety, power, and worth
- Habits, fears, addictions
- Sacred gifts: healing hands, strong intuition, creativity, resilience

- Unspoken pain and untold stories

Some are blessings. Some are burdens. All are invitations.

They invite you to:

- Continue what is wise
- Release what is heavy
- Transform what has never been healed
- And reclaim what was lost

You are the living altar of your bloodline. What passes through you… changes everything that came before and everything that will come after.

EPIGENETICS MEETS SPIRITUAL MEMORY

Science is beginning to validate what ancient mystics always knew: We inherit more than biology.

Through epigenetics, we now understand that trauma, fear, and emotional conditioning can be passed down in our DNA—encoded responses that live in the body long after the original event.

Spiritually, this means:

- Your fear may not be yours—it may be inherited.
- Your anxiety might be the echo of someone who lived in survival mode.
- Your guilt may be the residue of a story untold by a grandmother or great-grandfather.
- Your strength might be a sacred inheritance.

Healing isn't just personal—it's ancestral.

When you release something within yourself, the vibration shifts for those who came before and those who will come after. This is sacred alchemy.

SOUL MEMORY: THE REMEMBRANCE BEYOND THIS LIFE

Your soul is ancient. It carries the memory of:

- Past lives
- Soul agreements
- Sacred training in temples, stars, or spirit realms
- Lessons learned across time and timelines

Sometimes, when you enter a place you've never been but feel deeply familiar… Or meet someone and feel as if you've known them forever… Or have irrational fears or talents you can't explain… That's soul memory speaking.

It doesn't always appear as vivid past life recall. Often, it shows up as:

- Patterns that repeat with no known origin
- Emotional responses that seem *"too big."*
- Dreams that carry instructions
- Longings for places, practices, or times you can't name

When you pay attention to soul memory, you begin to remember your remarkable story transcending time, identity, and logic.

WHY YOU CHOSE THIS LINE, THIS LIFE, THIS TIME

Before birth, your soul chose this incarnation—not as punishment, but as alignment.

You chose:

- This family
- This body
- This time in history
- This set of inherited codes Because you knew you had the frequency to transform them.

You are not here by chance. You are here by design.

You are the one who said,

"I will remember. I will break what must be broken. I will heal what must be healed. I will carry the wisdom forward."

You are the breaker of cycles The weaver of new timelines The liberator of your line

And you are doing it… one vibration at a time.

THE PRACTICE OF ANCESTRAL HEALING

You don't need to know your full genealogy to heal. You only need to listen.

Here's a sacred practice to begin:

1. **Create an Ancestral Space**
   Sit quietly. Light a candle. Say aloud:
   "I honor the ones who came before me. I am listening."
2. **Ask:** What Am I Carrying That Isn't Mine?
   Write. Feel. Let memories rise. What fears, beliefs, or patterns feel old? Where might they have come from?
3. **Speak to Your Ancestors**
   Even those you never knew. Even those who were harmed. Say:

"I see you. I thank you. I release what no longer serves."

4. **Call Forth the Gifts**
   Ask:
   "What gifts have I inherited that I am ready to claim?" Healing hands, spiritual insight, survival strength—feel them in your body.
5. **Declare the Shift**
   Say:
   "The cycle ends with me. I choose love. I choose light. I choose liberation—for all of us."
   This is not about blaming or idolizing. It's about becoming a clear channel so the line can breathe again.

YOU ARE THE SACRED INTERSECTION

You are the intersection between:

- Ancestry and Legacy
- Memory and possibility
- Lineage and liberation

You are not repeating the story. You are rewriting it.

You are not trapped in karma. You are here to transcend it.

You are not a victim of your bloodline. You are its evolution.

You are the one your ancestors dreamed would come. You are the voice that sings where theirs were silenced. You are the healer of wounds they did not know how to name. You are the medicine. You are the code.

AFFIRMATIONS FOR ANCESTRAL HEALING AND SOUL MEMORY

- *"I carry the wisdom of my ancestors, and I choose what I keep."*
- *"I release what no longer serves my soul or my line."*
- *"I remember the lives I've lived, and I honor the soul I've become."*
- *"I walk with ancient knowing and future grace."*
- *"I am the living altar of my lineage. I choose healing, light, and legacy."*

REFLECTION & ACTIVATION

Ask yourself: What patterns am I here to end? What sacred gifts live in my bloodline? What soul memory is asking to rise within me now? What future do I want my descendants to inherit—energetically and emotionally?

You are not just one life. You are a portal for many.

Let the remembering begin.

LINEAGE HEALING PRAYER

For Honoring the Past, Healing the Present, and Blessing the Future

I call upon the Light.

I call upon the breath of Source that lives within me, the sacred code that chose this life, this bloodline, this moment in time.

I open my heart to those who came before me— known and unknown, named and unnamed. I acknowledge your pain. I bless your strength. I see what was not seen. I speak what was silenced. I forgive what was broken.

I choose to heal not from judgment, but from compassion. Not from fear, but from wisdom.

I release the cords of suffering passed down in silence. I return fear, shame, guilt, and suppression to the earth, transmuted in light.

I honor the gifts—the intuition, resilience, tenderness, truth— the sacred essence hidden in the lineage. I bring it forward, whole and radiant.

Let the pain end here. Let the wisdom rise now. Let this line be renewed, by choice and by love.

To my ancestors: I do not carry your burdens, but I carry your light. I am the healing. I am the song. I am the sacred turning point.

From this moment forward, I choose to live as the bridge— between what was and what can now be.

Amen. So it is. So it shall continue.

CHAPTER FOURTEEN

EPIGENETICS MEETS SPIRITUAL MEMORY

There is a wisdom in your blood that predates your name. A memory in your bones that was not written by your mind. A signal in your cells that carries echoes from lifetimes and lineages past.

You are not just the result of your choices. You are the continuation of a vibrational story—written in spirit, remembered in flesh.

Now, modern science is catching up to what the mystics have whispered for millennia: You inherit more than traits. You inherit experience. Emotion. Memory. Imprint.

And if it was passed to you—then it can be healed through you.

ENCODED IN THE BODY

Epigenetics teaches us that we do not live within the limits of our DNA. Instead, DNA is a script, and your environment—emotional, mental, spiritual—determines what parts of that script get activated or silenced.

In other words, your body remembers stories it never lived—because someone before you did.

- A child may fear abandonment without ever being left.
- A woman may carry shame in her womb that was never hers to carry.
- A man may feel the urge to hide his voice, though he's never been silenced.

Why? Because trauma doesn't die. It transfers—until someone transforms it.

That someone is often you.

THE EMOTIONAL IMPRINT LOOP

Here's what happens across time:

1. An ancestor experiences trauma (war, exile, grief, betrayal, poverty).
2. Their nervous system adapts: they become hypervigilant, quiet, reactive, emotionally numb, etc.
3. These adaptations get encoded into their biology—passed to the next generation.
4. You are born carrying those adaptations, even if the original story is never told.

But it doesn't stop there. You have the consciousness they didn't. The emotional language they lacked. The tools, support, and awareness to rewrite the loop.

You are the pattern breaker. The loop closer. The light bringer.

SCIENCE AND SOUL, HAND IN HAND

What happens when we blend epigenetic knowledge with spiritual truth?

We realize that healing is not just possible—it is programmable. We learn that spiritual practices—breathwork, intention, forgiveness, ritual, meditation—can physically alter gene expression.

You are not stuck with what you've been given. You are the editor of the ancestral script. And the more consciously you live, the more consciously your cells respond.

When you speak lovingly to yourself, you soothe generations. When you dance your grief, you release what was once unspeakable. When you forgive, you reprogram your lineage.

This is not abstract. This is vibrational science.

THE ECHOES OF SURVIVAL

If you've ever asked, *"Why do I feel this way, when nothing's wrong?"* Consider this:

- Your nervous system may be reacting to something your ancestors survived.
- Their fears might be echoing through you, asking for closure.
- Their silence may be asking you to speak.

This is not weakness. It is an invitation. To become aware. To step in as the conscious bridge between the past and the future.

What could not be processed then… can now be transformed through your awareness.

THE KEY: SAFE EXPRESSION

The original trauma may have been born in silence. So healing must begin with expression.

The body wants to speak. The soul wants to be heard.

You don't need to relive the pain to release it. You only need to let energy move:

- Cry without apology
- Breathe with presence
- Move your body in rhythm

- Speak the words your grandmother never could
- Write letters to ancestors who never had a voice
- Burn old beliefs in fire and let new ones rise

Movement heals memory. Expression clears entanglement. Witnessing sets it free.

STRENGTH IS ALSO INHERITED

You didn't just inherit trauma. You inherited resilience. Love. Wisdom. Medicine.

- The woman who endured but never gave up—you carry her grit.
- The healer who was silenced—you carry their gifts.
- The visionary who dreamed in secret—you carry their vision, finally free.

Let yourself claim the light in your lineage. Speak the names of the strong. Call forth the talents. Let them live through your hands, your art, your choices.

Your healing doesn't erase them—it completes them.

A NEW FUTURE BEGINS WITH YOU

When you shift the vibration of your own life, you shift it for the seven generations before and the seven to come.

You are not alone in your healing. Ancestors surround you, whispering, *"Thank you."* And future ones singing, *"We are free because of you."*

You were not given this path by accident. You were chosen by the line—because you are strong enough, wise enough, and encoded with the memory of how to set it all right.

And when the healing begins with you… it radiates in all directions.

AFFIRMATIONS FOR CELLULAR AND ANCESTRAL REPROGRAMMING

- *"I release what no longer belongs to me or my line."*
- *"I speak what was once silenced and bring peace to my blood."*
- *"Every breath I take heals those who came before me."*
- *"I awaken strength encoded in my DNA."*
- *"My body is a bridge, my soul is the light, and my life is the turning point."*

REFLECTION & ACTIVATION

Ask yourself: What emotion or fear feels ancient in me? What have I inherited that I am ready to transform? What strength is quietly asking to be claimed from my ancestry? What new vibration am I passing forward through my healing?

Write a letter to your lineage. Or to your body. Or to the child who will one day carry your frequency forward.

Because one day, they will look back and say:

"It changed with her." "It healed through him." "They were the light."

And they'll be right. Because you are not just the recipient of your inheritance— You are the rebirth of it.

CHAPTER FIFTEEN

THE REMEMBERING

You didn't come here to learn the code. You came to remember it.

Because everything you've read, everything you've felt while turning these pages, was already inside you. Not a lesson. A reminder.

You are not becoming. You are returning—to the light of your soul, the rhythm of your breath, the geometry of your being, and the purpose written in your DNA before time began.

And now, at the close of this book, you stand not at the end—but at the center. The center of your truth. The center of your power. The center of the Infinite Code.

WHAT YOU'VE REMEMBERED

This journey has not been linear. It's been spiralic—unfolding like the double helix of your soul.

Let's walk it back—not to repeat it, but to witness how far you've come:

- You learned that sound, breath, and intention are sacred instruments of creation.
- You uncovered the codes hidden in your voice, your body, your emotions.
- You activated the pyramid within you and discovered how thought becomes form.
- You aligned with the grid of the Earth and the stars, realizing you're not separate—you're part of the whole.

- You understood your relationships not as obstacles but mirrors—reflections of your energy, calling you higher.
- You explored the ancestral stream, healing what was passed down and reclaiming your right to rise.
- You met your soul memory, your frequency, your mission—and you said yes.

This is not light work. It is life work. And you are ready.

YOU ARE THE CODE

The Infinite Code is not just a truth. It is a frequency—a living, breathing intelligence flowing through all things.

It speaks through nature, numbers, colors, dreams, emotions, breath, memory, sound, symbols, and soul.

But most of all, it speaks through you.

You are the embodiment of divine intelligence. You are what happens when Stardust remembers it is conscious. When vibration takes form. When Spirit chooses to walk in a human body and shine anyway.

You are not a seeker anymore. You are remembered.

THE WORLD NEEDS YOUR LIGHT

This book was not just for your healing. It was an activation—because when one person awakens, the whole field shifts.

Now that you've remembered who you are:

- Speak your truth—not with force, but with clarity.

- Heal gently—not by fixing others, but by embodying coherence.
- Create consciously—not just for success, but for alignment.
- Love deeply—not to earn worth, but to express your wholeness.
- Rest when needed—not as weakness, but as sacred integration.
- Walk as light—not in perfection, but in presence.

You are not here to convince the world of your worth. You are here to transmit it. And you already are.

LIVING THE SPIRAL

Healing is not a straight line. Ascension is not a ladder. Your life will spiral—again and again—through:

- Remembering and forgetting
- Alignment and resistance
- Expansion and integration

This is not failure. It's fractal intelligence. You return to each lesson from a higher octave—deeper, clearer, wiser.

Each time you spiral, the light gets stronger. Each time you return, the code activates more fully. Each time you rise, you rise for all who came before you—and all who will come after.

WHAT NOW?

The Code Was Never Just Words. It Was a Call to Rise.

You don't need more information. You need more integration.

You don't need more doing. You need more being.

Let this book live in your breath, not just on your shelf. Let it guide the way you show up in the smallest moments— because that's where the codes awaken.

Let it shape:

- your rituals, so they become soul-grounding
- your relationships, so they become truth-reflecting
- your rest, so it becomes healing
- your voice, so it becomes activating
- your silence, so it becomes sacred
- your joy, so it becomes contagious
- your presence, so it becomes your offering to the world

This is not the end of a journey. It is the beginning of your becoming.

You are no longer the seeker. You are the signal.

THE WORLD HAS BEEN WAITING FOR YOU TO REMEMBER

There is a reason you found these words now. A reason they stirred something deep in your chest— like a forgotten melody returning home.

Because the part of you that holds the code… has always known.

And now it whispers:

"I remember who I am." "I remember why I came." "I remember the code... and I choose to live it."

You are not here to wait. You are here to activate. You are not here to prepare. You are here to embody.

Not someday. Not after you've healed everything. Not when the world is ready. Now.

You are the one. You are the light. You are the frequency the Earth has been waiting for.

FINAL AFFIRMATIONS FOR THE AWAKENED SOUL

Let these be your declarations. Your vibrational compass. Your return to truth—again and again.

- *"I am the living expression of the Infinite Code."*
- *"I remember the divine pattern within me, and I choose to live it."*
- *"I walk in alignment with grace, power, and purpose."*
- *"I allow my frequency to uplift the world around me."*
- *"I am no longer seeking—I am becoming."*
- *"My thoughts are intentional. My words are spells. My presence is sacred."*
- *"I am home in myself. And I am just getting started."*

FINAL REFLECTION & SOUL DECLARATION

Let this be more than journaling. Let this be your vow to the universe. Speak it. Feel it. Let your body resonate with it.

Write from your soul:

I am… I believe… I release… I welcome… I vow to remember… And I now choose to…

This is not an affirmation. This is a frequency shift. This is a soul declaration.

Seal it with presence. Speak it into the field. Because the field is listening.

And it responds not to your hopes— but to your embodied truth.

ONE LAST WHISPER

You came into this life carrying a question. You lived it. You wrestled with it. You danced with it. And now…

You have become the answer.

You came to remember the code. But it was never just a concept. It was never just a mystery to be solved.

It was the truth of who you are, waiting to be lived out loud.

And now… you are living it.

In your breath. In your choices. In your stillness. In your voice. In your love.

So let the remembering continue— in everything you touch, everything you bless, and everything you become.

You are not the ending. You are the beginning. You are the living code in motion.

And so it is. And so you are.

THE INFINITE CODE

CERTIFICATE OF COMPLETION

This certifies that

____

has completed the journey ocof
remembering and activation.

You are the infinite code.

MORE BY TINA KETCH

If The Infinite Code spoke to your soul, these titles will expand your light even further:

The Secrets to Life

A timeless spiritual guide that unveils the wisdom hidden in everyday experiences. Simple truths. Big shifts. A must-read for the awakening soul.

Transform Your Life in 30 Days

Your daily step-by-step path to transformation. Packed with empowering reflections, actions, and vibrations to realign your energy and reset your life.

The Breath That Becomes You

A sacred manuscript exploring the mystical intelligence of breath, alchemy, sacred geometry, and divine transformation. A spiritual activation in every chapter.

Vibrational Healing: A Journey of Scent, Remedy, and Sound

Explore the healing power of frequency, aroma, and resonance. Includes Solfeggio frequencies, emotional clearing techniques, and ancestral tones.

Behold, All Things New: A Modern Interpretation of the Book of Revelation

A bold, loving reinterpretation of Revelation—as a story of transformation, hope, and divine renewal. Written to inspire, not intimidate.

Sacred Speech: Aligning Words with Purpose

Thoughts are spells. Speech is energy. Learn to wield your words like a sacred wand and reshape your world through conscious language.

The Journey of Life Through the Zodiac Legacy (12-book series)

Each sign explored as a soul journey—traits, destiny, vibrational resonance, and unique healing paths. Includes:

- The Pisces Legacy
- The Leo Legacy
- The Virgo Legacy
- The Gemini Legacy
- And more...

What It Means Series (18 Titles)

Deep reflections on human, spiritual, and emotional truth. Includes:

- What It Means to Experience Life
- What It Means to Forgive Yourself
- What It Means to Understand Omnipresence
- What It Means to Be What You Eat
- And many more…

Your Journey to Light

A luminous guide for those seeking healing, clarity, and vibrational alignment with their purpose.

Beyond

A soul's journey through life, death, and rebirth. For anyone who's faced loss and wondered what lies beyond the veil.

www.ingramcontent.com/pod-product-compliance
Lightning Source LLC
LaVergne TN
LVHW010920110826
845149LV00013B/2436

* 9 7 9 8 9 9 2 8 2 5 4 4 2 *